*Music, Art, and Drama Experiences*
*for the Elementary Curriculum*

# Music, Art, and Drama Experiences for the Elementary Curriculum

## Lynne K. List

Professor Emeritus
College of the Virgin Islands

**Teachers College, Columbia University**
**New York and London**        **1982**

Published by Teachers College Press, 1234 Amsterdam Avenue,
New York, N.Y. 10027

**Library of Congress Cataloging in Publication Data**

List, Lynne K., 1931–
  Music, art, and drama experiences for the elementary
curriculum.

  Bibliography: p. 196
  Includes index.
  1. Arts—Study and teaching (Elementary)—United States.
NX304.L57     372.5     81-14575
                   AACR2


ISBN 0-8077-2696-6


Illustrated by Lorayne McGovern
Manufactured in the United States of America

87  86  85  84  83  82    1  2  3  4  5  6

*To Lew*

*Who waited so patiently*

# Contents

# Preface

This book is intended for classroom teachers and for prospective teachers. It presents creative methods for integrating music, art, and drama into the curriculum. Included are experiences and activities in the arts that can be used as teaching tools in the language arts, science, mathematics, and social studies areas. Incorporating the arts into the instructional program will allow teachers to enhance and stimulate the various subject areas. At the same time, children are helped to develop an understanding and appreciation of the aesthetic disciplines, which are often neglected in the regular classroom program.

No specific training, knowledge, or skills in music, art, or drama are needed by the classroom teacher to utilize and apply the experiences presented in this book, which represent unique and exciting ways to teach content materials.

It is important for teachers to become familiar with ways to use the arts in their classrooms. With the advent of educational budget limitations, specialists in the arts frequently are no longer available in school systems. If classroom teachers do not incorporate these disciplines, children may receive no exposure to the arts at all. In addition, the mainstreaming of children necessitates that teachers adopt additional and new teaching techniques in order to motivate and reach those students who are having difficulty learning through traditional procedures.

This book is novel in that it relates every music, art, and drama experience to a specific curriculum area and to a particular skill, concept, or instructional objective within that area. Unusual and imaginative content is presented along with tried and true procedures. These are valuable to any educator responsible for the instruction of children and may be of particular import for those who are working with children with special needs.

In chapter 1, "The Arts in the Elementary Curriculum," the importance and relevance of the arts in the educational process are examined. Music, art, and drama are defined, and the contributions of the arts and their relationships to each of the curriculum areas are discussed. In addition, a number of suggestions are presented for using the arts with children with special needs.

Each of the following chapters is devoted to a particular curriculum area. In each, detailed and specific applications for teaching skills and concepts, using music, art, and drama experiences, are presented along with explanations of other relationships that exist.

The experiences, games, crafts, and projects presented are in no way intended to be all inclusive. They have been selected as examples of arts applications to the various curriculum, skill, and content areas. They serve as a basic foundation of activities that can be incorporated into the instructional program and serve as springboards for further creativity on the part of the teacher.

The activities have been categorized based on the definitions provided in chapter 1, but a great deal of overlapping exists among the different aesthetic disciplines. It is not possible to establish any one categorization system that will receive the unanimous support of each of the disciplines.

Even so, the activities are categorized as music, art, or drama. No levels or gradations of difficulty have been assigned. Children must be related to where they are, and their grade placements frequently are not commensurate with their instructional levels. This is particularly true in the case of children with special needs. In addition, a child's ability in one art form may be at a higher or lower level from ability in another art form. It is impossible to establish an order that will serve the needs of every teacher, in every situation, for every type of child.

Many activities described are applicable to more than one curriculum or skill or content area. To avoid redundancy, each activity is listed under one area only, with reference made to other applicable areas.

Citations are provided for all activities taken directly from other sources as well as for activities merely suggested by projects listed in other sources. In many instances, the original sources simply described the activity and made no reference to a subject area or skill area to which the activity could be directed most profitably. The relationships established, therefore, in a large number of cases were those interpreted or inferred by the author.

This book should be of invaluable assistance in providing experiences in the arts the classroom teacher can incorporate into the daily instructional program. Happy Teaching!

*Music, Art, and Drama Experiences*
*for the Elementary Curriculum*

# CHAPTER 1

# The Arts in the Elementary Curriculum

## OVERVIEW

ALL CHILDREN need to express themselves creatively. They prefer to be participants rather than spectators. Children enjoy painting more than looking at artworks. They like playing an instrument more than listening to an orchestra. In short, arts activities have a natural appeal for children.

The function of the arts in education, however, often is misunderstood. The many genres of music, art, and drama are not simply forms of entertainment, something nice but not necessary or edifying. They are far more than just special subjects offered for talented children. The arts serve as tools to express feelings, to respond to particular situations, and to enhance learning in all aspects of the general curriculum. In addition, they assist in the development of cognition and emphasize the development of abilities in divergent (many correct answers) rather than convergent (one correct response) thinking.

There are those who regard only work specifically oriented to cognitive development as important (King, 1975, p. 76). It is this attitude, however, that has stifled the basic creative impulse and narrowed the potential contribution of the arts in education. Eisner (1980) details the importance of the arts in the development of cognition. Cognition, he states, develops through all the senses. Each sense modality provides a different focus for life's variable experiences. Abstract sensory concepts are developed through concrete experiences. This abstraction process

1

exemplifies the constructive use of cognition and is at the root of the arts and types of knowing. The ability to construct and conceptualize in each modality does not simply develop maturationally. It must be trained, and the child's environment plays an important part in its training (pp. 2, 3). One must be trained to see aesthetically, to hear musically, or to respond dramatically.

If language is a vehicle for expression, then the arts must be considered as a language since they, just as mathematics and oral and written language, have a syntax, a grammar, and an architecture of organization (p. 4). Each of the artistic symbol systems informs and assists in forming the mind. It is through them that one inquires. In addition, illiteracy in any of the major systems represents a deprivation of some kind of understanding (pp. 4, 5). A description of a flower or a song provides one way to convey what the flower or song is like. A picture of the flower or seeing the sheet music provides a second way. Sniffing the aroma of the flower or listening to the song played provides a third way. Each method provides for a segment of the total from its own vantage point.

The Organizations for the Essentials of Education, in a brochure entitled *The Essentials of Education* (undated), stress that a central concept of the essentials of education is the interdependence of skills and concepts and that the essentials include, among other things, the ability of individuals to express themselves through the arts and to understand other people's artistic expression. The organizations call for all disciplines to come together and to recognize and to acknowledge their interdependence. Twelve professional associations endorsed the statement on the essentials of education. Included among them are the American Alliance for Health, Physical Education, Recreation and Dance; the Music Educators National Conference; the National Art Education Association; and the Speech Communication Association. They were joined by associations representing such content areas as foreign languages, reading, social studies, English, mathematics, and science.

The Arts in General Education Program (AGE) emphasizes the integration rather than the isolation of the arts in the general curriculum. The program includes two functions of particular import. It maintains that the arts program serves the needs of all types of exceptionalities and that, emmeshed with other subjects, it enhances, by enlivening, general education (Fowler, 1978, p. 31).

The arts can indeed be used with all kinds of exceptional children. Coleman (1964) describes how to work successfully, using movement and over twenty different instruments, with children who are visually, aurally, or orthopedically handicapped and those who are educable and trainable mentally retarded. Since music, art, and drama activities emphasize process, they are clearly advantageous procedures for use with gifted and talented students too.

The arts contribute to human mental, psychological, and physical development (Fowler, 1978, p. 32). This is facilitated by the use of all the senses in the learning process.

Basic learnings can be stimulated with arts processes since coding and decoding are involved in each art form. Each art form represents a different symbolic system that the students use expressively (Fowler, 1978, p. 32). Art is the language the artist uses to communicate with others. Music is the language the composer or performer uses to speak with others. Drama is the language the thespian or entertainer uses to speak with others.

There are those who feel that care should be exercised when the arts are integrated into the school program. They contend that the integrity of the arts experience should be maintained within the context with which it is integrated and that, though the arts can be used as teaching-learning tools in the curriculum areas, their unique properties should not be sacrificed. Wankleman et al. (1973, p. 4) emphasize that the arts should be used as more than just a reporting device, that the art form should not become a slave to another subject thereby destroying its essence and making it no longer one of the arts.

Classroom teachers, however, who generally are not specialists in one or more of the art forms, are not concerned solely with artistic or aesthetic experiences. Though some of their lessons are intended to present genuine arts qualities, much of their instruction uses the art form merely as a teaching tool, as a springboard for motivating students by providing a different approach to traditional instructional methodology.

The experiences, games, crafts, and projects contained in this book fall into both categories. Those intended as artistic or aesthetic experiences retain the identity of the art form and permit it to operate on its own principles rather than those of the subject being studied. Those activities that use the art form as a method or medium for teaching something else fall into the category of games, crafts, and projects.

"The validity of an activity does not reside in the activity itself, but in the meaning it has for the child" (Crosscup, 1966, p. 3). The purpose for using the arts in education is not limited to the training of artists, the production of performers, or the developing of an appreciation for the arts. Arts activities are frequently employed as devices to stimulate learning. They are the "spoonful of sugar" to make the learning more palatable. They can serve as a means to some other end as well as an end in themselves.

What is meant by music, art, and drama experiences? Some disagreement will be found, and no one set of definitions will be acceptable to all disciplines since there are many overlapping areas. Drama books frequently include set design, costuming, makeup, and dance—areas that might be claimed by art and music. Puppetry can be found in both art and drama books. The following definitions are used in this book for the purpose of categorizing the arts experiences. In addition, the value of each of the particular arts is discussed.

## Music Experiences

Music includes dancing, singing, composers, performers, instruments, performing, harmony, melody, and written music of all kinds.

The Department of Education, State of Florida (1977), notes six reasons why music should be included in the school program. First, it is an aid in achieving basic skills. Second, it serves as a major force in moral and ethical education. Third, it helps to develop student self-image and personal traits. Fourth, it has relevance in that the skills are usable immediately, and it also permits for real-life exposures through performances at community clubs and social events. Fifth, it promotes physical development and health. Last, it assists in refining basic sense perceptions. To support the statements, a number of studies are cited whose findings indicate the validity of the advantages.

Another reason for including music in the school program is that, since children require repetition for learning, the use of repeated muscular memory activities accelerates the learning process (Nash et al., 1977, p. 3). Music can be used easily as the means to integrate holistic and analytic strategies.

Still another reason is that music relates to the type of activity to which the youth of today are accustomed. In addition, with the advent of more and more hours of television watching, children have become quite inactive. Inactivity breeds lethargy in mind and body (Nash et al., 1977, "Introduction"). Music gets children to move again, something they need to do if they are to learn.

Further, since music activities involve motion, methods of exploration and problem solving are utilized. There is a high degree of pupil involvement. The learning experience entails elements of time, space, force, flow, etc., and helps to develop coordination.

## Art Experiences

Art encompasses such areas as painting, drawing, collage, architecture, sculpture, fashion, costuming, photography, artists, and advertising.

Children at all levels of development can participate in and enjoy art experiences. Human beings have used art as a method of communication since the beginning of time, and art still remains one of the links that is used and understood universally (Taylor, et al., 1970, p. vii).

Kranz and Deley (1970, p. 7) discuss the values of art instruction programs. They indicate that creative manipulation of flexible materials is necessary both to early developmental training and to the structuring of healthy learning skills and attitudes. In addition, art activities allow children to progress at their own paces and are easily expandable to other areas of study. Therefore they nurture the desire to learn. Art experiences also allow for children to study and master their environments. Since the basic skills and subjects can be taught through art, art has a proven value in remedial instruction and, as such, is a viable instructional procedure in educationally deprived urban areas.

Taylor et al. (1970, p. viii) identify the following goals of art programs:

1. The arts develop creativity in children.
2. Art experiences assist in the development of intelligent consumers and producers.
3. Cooperative endeavors and social adjustments result from participation in group art activities.
4. The visual experiences promote the growth and development of the child.
5. Art activities and experiences provide for the release of emotions and feelings.

## Drama Experiences

Drama includes pantomime, improvisation, plays, puppetry, movement, speech, and performers.

Drama can be regarded as one of the arts along with, and equal to, music and art. When drama is taught as an art, both child development and learning will be affected (Siks, 1975, pp. 7–8).

Creative drama differs from children's theater in that drama is concerned with participant experiences while theater involves what one watches, where the communication occurs between the actors and the audience and among those who are acting. An excellent definition is offered by Crosscup (1966, p. 31). He states that creative dramatics is "the extension of the child's make-believe, through adult help, to a content which expands the child's horizon in cultural and human terms."

Drama experiences have many values. They involve concentration, the use of all the senses, imagination, the physical self, speech, emotion, and intellect (Way, 1967, p. 14). In addition, doing drama permits children to experiment with ways to respond to particular situations.

Two components of drama often neglected in the curriculum are puppetry and movement. Though the making of puppets could be included in the art area, the use of them is exclusively the province of drama. They are therefore included in this area.

Puppets are loved by children and adults alike. Not only are they potent tools for instruction in all areas, but they also offer the opportunity to incorporate other art forms. Music can be added easily to a script; costuming and set design are important to the drama; and playwriting is an essential element. The use of puppets has the following values as well: (1) shy, retiring, and insecure students often can overcome their timidity and gain assurance since it is the puppet, not they, who is performing, (2) children who have been experiencing failure can be successful in this area, (3) the group work is advantageous for learning to work cooperatively (4) poor readers receive reinforcement as a group works to prepare a story for presentation, (5) aesthetic satisfaction is gained from the creativeness of the activity, (6) the approach emphasizes learning by doing, and (7) creative interpretation is fostered.

Puppetry is an ancient art that predates written history. Primitive societies used hinged masks and jointed skulls for religious ceremonies and magical rites. As long ago as four thousand years, puppets with moveable limbs were developed. By the second century B.C., stringed puppets were performing in Egypt. Puppet theaters were an established art form from the time of the Greeks until the present.

During the Middle Ages, puppet marionettes performed in religious dramas and mystery plays. The word "marionette" is thought by some to come from a literal translation of "Little Marion," a diminutive for the Virgin Mary. Others believe its etymology is *marotte*, which means "fool's scepter." The religious puppet plays were very popular during the fourteenth and fifteenth centuries. By the seventeenth century, marionette operas became popular. Joseph Haydn even wrote several marionette operas in the 1700s. Over the years, millions of people have been exposed to the wonder and joy of puppetry.

Movement activities allow for individuals to give a form to their feelings, attitudes, and ideas. Children must first learn to identify their own feelings or emotions before they can learn to be cognizant of the feelings of others. Children must learn also how to work with other people. This discovery combines with intellectual pursuits to enrich the entire learning process. King (1975, pp. 17, 18) cites an example of the application of these learnings to a social studies unit of study, "The Role of Immigration in the Development of the United States." She says that the students would first have to consider the answer to such questions as, "What would a person need to feel before leaving the known for the unknown? How might these feelings have developed? How would it feel to live in a strange country where no one spoke your language?"

Movement activities also are related to fine and gross motor coordination and can be used to teach skills and to develop concepts in all the curriculum areas. Since children are less inhibited than adults and enjoy these movements, these activities are particularly good.

## CONTRIBUTIONS OF THE ARTS TO THE CURRICULUM

Integrating music, art, and drama into the curriculum is a unique and fascinating educational procedure for teachers and a breath of fresh air for students. The arts can be used to improve education in the basics by serving as learning instruments in almost all subject areas: the language arts (oral and written language, and reading), mathematics, science, and the social studies. Utilizing the art forms in creative ways, integrating rather than isolating the arts, provides many advantages.

1. Various subjects can be enhanced and learning can be stimulated. By providing a radical change from the typical procedures, and by virtue of the materials involved, the arts provide for an immediate interest on the part of children. In addition, they supply an extension of learning that could not be obtained in any other way. The unique techniques serve as motivational devices for most students, including the so-called disinterested learner.

2. The backgrounds of pupils can be enriched. By integrating the arts, the teacher is exposing the students to areas about which they otherwise might never have known. These exposures allow the children to bring greater learning experiences to each new learning situation.

3. New avenues of learning are provided. The arts furnish a vehicle of learning for children with academic and special educational problems. Not only are the experiences easily incorporated into educational and therapeutic programs for all types of students, but they also are particularly adaptable to programs designed for exceptional students. Nash et al. (1977, p. 2) explain that cognitive learning is directed mainly to the left side of the brain, where language, logic, and reasoning take place. Children, though, do not react in the same way as adults. They direct their learning more to the right side of the brain. (See figure 1-1.) This side deals with motor-muscular activities, spatial orientation, artistic endeavors, imagination, feelings. School programs should combine language and reasoning with sensory and motor activities so that an integra-

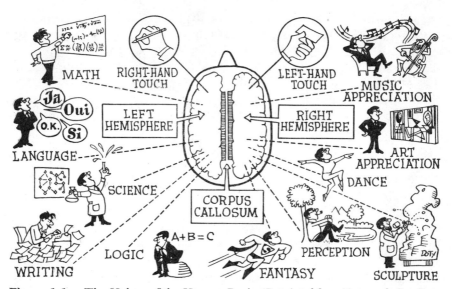

**Figure 1-1.**   The Halves of the Human Brain (*Reprinted from Newsweek, Roy Doty, artist*)

tion takes place that allows for learning in such areas as reading and mathematics.

Weinstein (1980, p. 23) explains that the differences between normal children and those with developmental dyscalculia (disorder in doing arithmetic) is that the child who has undue difficulty in mathematics has a slower development of the analytical left cerebral hemisphere. Children who lag in the development of logical thought persist in relying on holistic cognitive strategies. As a result, they have difficulty with such things as counting, place values, and conservation of area and of volume, which require analytical thinking (p. 25). She suggests that these children be encouraged to think analytically, be given tasks where the solution may be arrived at through spatial processing, and be given instant feedback on their successes (p. 28).

The arts can be used easily as the means for integrating holistic strategies with the analytic ones. This occurs whenever an artistic activity is used to facilitate the development of an analytic one. For example, children move to music as the strains make them feel. They then analyze why they felt that way and what occurred in the music to elicit the particular feelings.

4. The arts may be an area of strength for children with language problems. The opportunity to express oneself through media other than oral or written language affords a tremendous benefit to many students.

5. Psychological satisfaction can be obtained. Children who are hav-

ing difficulty in the traditional academic areas with the conventional teaching approaches have an opportunity to do well in the arts, to succeed, and even to excel.

6. An appreciation and understanding of aesthetic disciplines is developed. This appreciation will stand children in good stead for the remainder of their lives.

7. The arts serve to improve education in specific skills that underlie all areas of learning. These skills are following directions, developing attention span, interpreting symbols, coordinating muscles, concentrating, and listening. The arts, and music in particular, reinforce these specific areas of learning (Reichard and Blackburn, 1973, p. 9).

8. Self-discovered, self-appropriated learning significantly influences behavior. When students participate in learning, they assume a greater responsibility for it (Rogers, 1969, pp. 162–163). The use of all the senses in the learning process provides for self-propelled learning experiences.

9. The teaching procedure utilizes all the senses. This technique is referred to frequently as the "multisensory" or "multimodal approach." This method is advocated particularly for children with certain types of special needs, including those who are hyperactive.

10. Teachers need not have specialized training. Though a background in the arts would be of value, the teacher need not have any special skills to be able to incorporate the arts into the school program.

## THE RELATIONSHIP OF THE ARTS TO CURRICULUM AREAS

All forms of the creative arts provide for especially good child-centered experiences that are adaptable to every aspect of the classroom program and to all skill areas.

### The Language Arts

The language arts consists of oral and written language and reading. Though art, music, and drama are adaptable to all aspects of the classroom program, they seem to have been accepted most readily, and have a more obvious relationship, in the language arts program. This may be because the three art forms are used to communicate ideas, feelings, and moods.

Bookbinder (1965, pp. 783–85, 796) argues for the use of art in teaching all communication skills. He says that, historically, art has been used to communicate ideas and that art is a means of communication in young people that closely parallels the development of verbal expression. The alphabet itself was based on picture writing. Bookbinder also urges that educators remember the interrelationships of various means of expression in order to enrich one area by using the other.

McIntyre (1974, p. 6) contends that drama skills should be used as a technique for furthering all language learning. She also emphasizes that movement is important to language learning since a knowledge of how, why, when, and where movement takes place is necessary for a full understanding of language (p. 9).

Learning to code and decode is a natural outgrowth of the use of the arts processes. *Coding* involves perceiving, reacting, and creating. Fowler (1978, p. 32) suggests that a drawing of a house can lead children to see that there are other ways to picture a house and many words to describe it. Similarly, a piece of music or creative dramatics may lead children to realize that there are many ways to express mood and feeling. In any of the situations, vocabulary can be increased.

*Decoding* involves recreating, interpreting, and evaluating. Music, art, and drama permit one to decode and to interpret what others say through their works (Fowler, 1978, p. 32).

Singing is merely an extension of speech. Voice pitch, flexibility, and expression as well as proper pronunciation are developed in this area. Choral speaking, an extension of singing, fosters the same skills. Singing also helps one develop confidence in standing before a group, something many children, and adults, are afraid to do.

Listening skills are fostered through drama and music. Though listening is important to all areas, it is particularly significant in phonics and various reading skills. Listening abilities develop maturationally but listening skills do not always come naturally; they have to be trained. There is some disagreement over the meaning of the word "listening." To some, it refers to the hearing of sounds, particularly spoken sounds. To others, it includes attaching meaning to those sounds. To still others, it involves interpreting those sounds, which is a step beyond meaning. Listening, obviously, involves more than just hearing. In an attempt to refine the terminology, the word "auding" was proposed as a broader term that would include all aspects: hearing, listening to, and understanding spoken languge (Donoghue, 1975, p. 203). Listening is an art, and it can be developed, in all its aspects, through the creative arts.

Kean and Personke (1976, p. 377) believe that the lyrics of music can contribute to poetry study, that children can learn to discriminate among good and bad lyrics they hear and apply these learnings to the study of poetry. The lyrics of familiar music can also lead children to the writing of their own lyrics and, as an outgrowth, their own poetry. In the process they learn that lyrics are essentially poems set to music.

Many processing skills can be developed through music. Perceptual discrimination can be assisted in that there are shifts in rhythm stresses; tempos speed up and down; notes raise and lower, lengthen and shorten; and interval differences occur between notes. Music also assists in developing motor coordination, as do art and drama activities. All the arts promote such reading readiness skills as language development and listening skills (Talbott, 1980).

Many reading skills can be developed. Musical accenting can be used to teach syllabication. Vocabulary can be enriched. Learning the definitions of "staccato," "glissando," "crescendo," "accelerando," and "ritardando" assists children in appropriate responses and provides opportunities for vocabulary development. Concepts also can be developed as children are exposed to high/low, near/far, loud/soft, and so forth.

All the performing arts can be related to reading. Participation in the arts helps children to develop self-confidence, creativity, and an understanding of how to express what they feel.

Creative writing can be fostered. When melody, harmony, tone, rhythm, and form are taught, children learn to respond to mood and feelings, and these responses can be converted to oral and written expression. In addition, music has the power to release fantasy (Sendak, 1966, p. 202). It is through music that children and adults are able to express feelings that lie deeper than words (p. 202). This same music permits the creative impulses to surface and to be expressed in oral and written language. Creative art and dramatic work, and art and dramatic interpretations, also promote oral and written expression.

In summary, the arts relate to oral language through the development of such skills as vocabulary, listening, imagery, following directions, and speaking. In the written-language area, they can be an assist in developing skills in creative and expository writing, grammar, and spelling. In reading, they can be an aid in such areas as the teaching of the alphabet, classification, concept development, details, main ideas, phonics, processing skills, and syllabication.

## Science

Art seems to have a greater relationship with science than do music or drama; however, in the areas where music and drama are applicable, the relationship is strong.

Art can be used to teach science as it relates to particular concepts. Such concepts as texture, color, pattern, space, shape, and form are only a few of the areas that can be developed. Observing natural and man-made shapes and forms in architecture, drawing, painting, and sculpture can lead one to think about such items as light, shadow, mass, and structure (Kennedy, 1978). Photography is a natural art form to be used in conjunction with these areas. In addition to developing concepts, specific topics can be explored. These include animals, plants, insects, inventions, nature, perception, physical changes, the solar system, stars, and the spectrum.

A number of art games can be played with groups of children. The scenario can come from such disciplines as biology, physics, or chemistry. The instructions for playing and inventing these games are involved but can be mastered easily by the average classroom teacher. Pavey (1980) describes these games in detail along with their merits.

Music, too, can be used to demonstrate a number of scientific concepts. In addition, the relationship of music to sound is obvious.

Quite a few songs exist that can be used to help teach such topics as health, plants, animals, and weather. The topics that seem most easily suited to musical activities include body parts, general health, inertia, action-reaction theory, nature, physical changes, and sounds.

Drama activities can accomplish the same objectives as music and art. Children can "act out," pantomime, or move to demonstrate or simulate various scientific concepts and facts. They can pretend to be animals or plants. They can manipulate body parts, show physical changes, and react to weather conditions. Drama activities are applicable to almost every area of science.

Each of the art forms has something unique to contribute to the science curriculum.

## Mathematics

The arts can assist in the development of mathematics skills and concepts. They can be used to teach mathematics as it relates to particular concepts. Through art, the concepts of shapes and forms can be developed. Drawing, painting, sculpture, and architecture can teach one to see natural and manmade shapes and forms (Kennedy, 1978). Art can also be used as a vehicle for teaching such mathematics basics as cardinal directions, counting, numbers, multiplication, graphs, measurement, symbols, fractions, proportions, and time.

Through music, a number of areas can be fostered. The number systems based on bases other than 10, relative numerical relationships, fractional concepts represented in rhythm problems, and skills in abstract symbolism are just a few of the areas. Time duration concepts can also be developed. The focus can be on duration of sounds, meter, tempo, or timed compositions. There are many other areas to which music can be applied. They include basic facts, measurement, money, parts, and shapes.

Drama experiences can be used to develop shape and form concepts, basic facts, and numerical relationships. Movement activities can be used to have the children experience the concepts of fast and slow as they relate to tempo. Children can learn symmetry by creating symmetrical shapes with their bodies, with partners, or with a group. Drama has much to offer in this area.

The various art forms have many applications to the mathematics program. The more one uses the art forms, the more the possibilities will present themselves. The applications are limited only by the imagination and creativity of the teacher.

## Social Studies

In social studies, the arts provide a means for learning history and are a key for understanding the ideas and concepts of other people and cultures. They provide visual pictures of people, places, events, and cultures in history that can be more illuminating than the printed word. Through folk songs and dances, through music of a country or period, history becomes alive. Through the interrelationships dealt with in drama, affective and cognitive learning goals can be both motivated and accelerated (Kelly, 1975, p. 110).

The arts provide an excitement and an emotional experience that are not found in the conventional social studies textbook, that cannot be obtained from the printed word. Further, the arts allow children to make contact with their own ideas and, in so doing, to understand themselves better (Cohen and Gainer, 1977). Folk music, singing, and dancing are particularly meaningful because children were a part of the original rituals, festivals, and occasions. Such music as Negro jazz, Scottish and Irish airs, American Indian ceremonial dances, African drum music, English folk carols, and Haitian carnival tunes are easily adaptable to the classroom program. In addition, map and graph work, the community, forms of government, and holidays can be taught through music.

Kraus (1975, pp. 128–29) emphasizes that history consists of more than simply a series of battles with winners and losers. It involves a progression of attitude changes. Students, for a rich understanding of history, must comprehend the feelings of the people of the time; their fears, anxieties, indecisions, and values. These learnings can be developed through drama experiences.

Fowler (1978, p. 30) describes a stimulating social studies lesson in which music, the visual arts, media, and drama were used as the tools for learning history. The occasion was Theodore Roosevelt's final press conference before leaving office. The student reporters had prepared questions for the president. The queries ranged from the Panama Canal to the shooting of McKinley, from the "Big Stick" policy to the first flying machine. Songs of the 1904 campaign and patriotic songs of the period were played and sung. The outcome was that the students were actively involved in the events of history and the experience was an exciting and emotional learning situation.

All the objectives of the social studies program, namely, humanistic, social, and intellectual, can be fostered through the arts.

## USING THE ARTS WITH CHILDREN WITH SPECIAL NEEDS

When working with children with special needs, some basic guidelines should be followed.

1. Establish as individualized a program as possible.
2. Begin with activities at a level each of the children can handle with ease, to ensure a successful experience.
3. Make provision for the children to be aware of their progress and their successes.
4. Provide meaningful experiences.
5. Teach one activity at a time. When activities are complex, they may have to be broken into smaller units.
6. Start with simple directions, one direction at a time initially, and add more as the children indicate a capability to handle them.
7. Work slowly. Requiring the children to respond quickly or to accomplish a great deal in a short period of time may be unrealistic.
8. Provide for repetition of learning. Children with special needs require more repetitions than the average learner.
9. Correct incorrect responses immediately, before a pattern is set firmly.
10. Eliminate as much pressure as possible. Far more will be accomplished if the atmosphere is relaxed and therefore conducive to learning.
11. Keep lessons fairly short in order to maximize the children's abilities to concentrate and to retain their attentiveness.
12. Alternate types of activities. A movement (active) activity should follow a sedentary one; an easy activity should follow one requiring more concentration or one that taxes cognitive functioning.
13. Conduct frequent reviews to reinforce the learnings.
14. Stimulate the children (motivate them) for each activity but do

not overmotivate. Intense stimulation may be so exciting that the children's emotional levels may interfere with their learning processes.
15. Encourage experimentation with many different kinds of materials and activities.

# REFERENCES

BOOKBINDER, JACK. "Art and Reading." *Language Arts* 52 (September 1965): 783–85, 796.

COHEN, ELAINE, AND GAINER, RUTH. "Art as Communication with Children." *Childhood Education* 53 (February 1977): 199–201.

COLEMAN, JACK L. *Music for Exceptional Children.* Evanston, Ill.: Sunny-Birchand Co., 1964.

CROSSCUP, RICHARD. *Children and Dramatics.* New York: Charles Scribner's Sons, 1966.

DEPARTMENT OF EDUCATION, STATE OF FLORIDA. *Why Music in Our Schools?* 1977.

DONOGHUE, MILDRED R. *The Child and the English Language Arts.* Dubuque, Iowa: William C. Brown, 1975.

EISNER, ELLIOT W. "The Role of the Arts in the Invention of Man." *New York University Education Quarterly* (Spring 1980): 2–7.

FOWLER, CHARLES. "Integral and Undiminished: The Arts in General Education." *Music Educators Journal* (January 1978): 30–33.

KEAN, JEAN, AND PERSONKE, CARL. *The Language Arts.* New York: St. Martin's Press, 1976.

KELLY, ELIZABETH FLORY. "Curriculum Dramatics." In *Children and Drama,* edited by Nellie McCaslin. New York: David McKay Co., 1975, pp. 109–27.

KENNEDY, WALLACE. "Local-Citywide Program." *Music Educators Journal* (January 1978): 46–48.

KING, NANCY. *Giving Form to Feeling.* New York: Drama Book Specialists/Publishers, 1975.

KRANZ, STEWART, AND DELEY, JOSEPH. *The Fourth "R": Art for the Urban School.* New York: Van Nostrand Reinhold Co., 1970.

KRAUS, JOANNA HALPERT. "Dramatizing History." In *Children and Drama,* edited by Nellie McCaslin. New York: David McKay Co., 1975, pp. 128–39.

MCINTYRE, BARBARA M. *Creative Drama in the Elementary School.* Itasca, Ill.: F. E. Peacock Publishers, 1974.

NASH, GRACE C.; JONES, GERALDINE W.; POTTER, BARBARA A.; AND SMITH, PATSY F. *The Child's Way of Learning.* Sherman Oaks, Calif.: Alfred Publishing Co., 1977.

ORGANIZATIONS FOR THE ESSENTIALS OF EDUCATION. *The Essentials of Education* (undated brochure)

PAVEY, DON. *Art-Based Games.* Denver: Love Publishing Co., 1980.

REICHARD, CARY L., AND BLACKBURN, DENNIS B. *Music Based Instruction for the Exceptional Child.* Denver: Love Publishing Co., 1973.

ROGERS, CARL R. *Freedom to Learn.* Columbus, Ohio: Charles E. Merrill Publishing Co., 1969.

SENDAK, MAURICE. "The Shaping of Music." In *Readings About Children's Literature,* edited by Evelyn R. Robinson. New York: David McKay Co., 1966, pp. 201–205.

SIKS, GERALDINE BRAIN. "Drama in Education—A Changing Scene." In *Children and Drama,* edited by Nellie McCaslin. New York: David McKay Co., 1975, pp. 1–12.

TALBOTT, GLADYS. "Learning to Read Through the Arts." *News for Parents from IRA.* Newark, Del.: International Reading Association, May 1980.

TAYLOR, FRANK D., ARTUSO, ALFRED A., AND HEWETT, FRANK M. *Creative Art Tasks for Children.* Denver: Love Publishing Co., 1970.

WANKLEMAN, WILLARD, WIGG, PHILLIP, AND WIGG, MARIETTA. *A Handbook of Arts and Crafts.* Dubuque, Iowa: William C. Brown Co., 1973.

WAY, BRIAN. *Development Through Drama.* London: Longman's, 1967.

WEINSTEIN, MARCIA L. "A Neuropsychological Approach to Math Disability." *New York University Education Quarterly* (Winter 1980): 22–28.

# CHAPTER 2

# Written-Language Experiences

THE EXPERIENCES IN THIS CHAPTER are presented in three broad skill categories: writing, grammar, and spelling.

## WRITING

Writing skills include both expository and creative writing. *Expository writing* refers to factual writing while *creative writing* is associated with literary forms involving the production of stories and imaginative works. The arts experiences for writing generally are applicable to both areas, with just slight variations.

### Music Experiences and Related Games, Crafts, and Projects

1. IMAGINATIVE THINKING*

MATERIALS: Record or cassette player, recording that evokes the desired feeling.

PROCEDURE: Discuss a topic, such as monsters, with a group of students. Talk about how monsters make one feel, what they look like, where they are found. Play a recording that evokes the ominous feeling of monsters. Then divide the children into groups of four to develop a story involving a monster of their own creation. The children must first write a good description of their monster. When each story is completed, the children determine a characteristic sound for their monster and what sound effects would be most appropriate, that is, what kind of sounds their monster would make. The children then create the sound effects using instruments, voices, or any other objects to produce the sounds:

clank: tin can and drumstick
"ow": slide whistle
thump: wood block
"eeek": voice

A Monster Quartet can be set up using the characteristic sounds of the monster in rhythmic patterns, as shown in figure 2–1. A chart of the patterns can be made and a conductor selected to keep the beat.

*Contributed by Barbara Stock, North Kingstown, R.I.

## 2. Expressing Feelings

MATERIALS: Record or cassette player, an instrumental recording.
PROCEDURE: Play an instrumental recording of a song with a catchy melody. After listening, the children discuss what feelings the music evoked: sadness, happiness, loneliness, and so forth. The children write compositions to express their feelings. The compositions are read aloud with the music as a background. More advanced children may be asked to write lyrics for the music, after which they would sing the song with the music.

## 3. Developing Creative Thinking

MATERIALS: Nothing special required.
PROCEDURE: Ask the children to compose an original poem based on

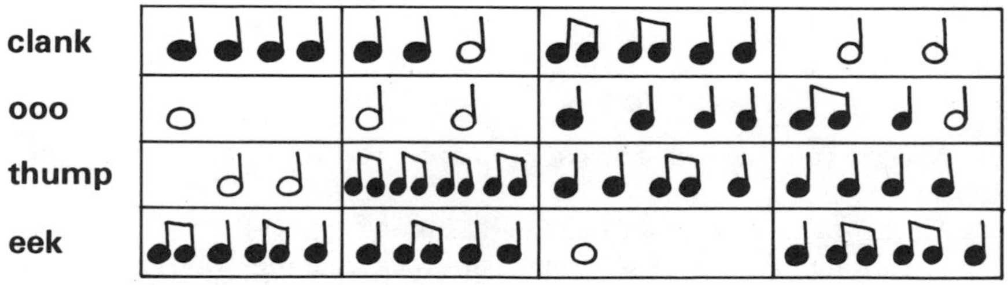

Figure 2-1

a given theme. When the poems are finished, the children are asked to write a melody to go with their poems. If they cannot actually write the melody, they simply compose a tune. The finished products are sung by the children.

## 4. Recreating Form*

MATERIALS:  A number of ballads of different types.

PROCEDURE:  After listening to and reading ballads of different types and studying the characteristics of the ballad, the children select and paraphrase one ballad. The children must retain the same form. The topics can be anything from an emotion to an account of history to a local news event. This activity is well suited for use in social studies.

*Contributed by Beverly Harrison, East Greenwich, R. I.

## 5. Analyzing Critically

MATERIALS:  Newly recorded song or a musical television show or live musical performance.

PROCEDURE:  After listening to a newly recorded song or viewing a musical TV show or live performance, the children are asked to write a review of the work. These reviews are then shared and compared. Professional reviews should be introduced so that the children can learn the elements contained in a good review.

## 6. Learning Form

MATERIALS:  Cut up sheet music of songs with which children are familiar and cut up compositions.

PROCEDURE:  Have the children liken musical form (beginning—middle—end) to written work. Mix up the parts of a musical piece and have the children compare these to a mixed-up composition. The children should learn that music, as writing, has specific elements that go into particular places.

## 7. Writing Factually

MATERIALS:  Biographies of composers, musicians, dancers.

PROCEDURE:  Have the children research the lives of musical personages of their choice. It may be preferable to use artists about whom the children are studying in the social studies program or have read in the reading program or to whose works they have been exposed recently.

The finished works must state facts only. No editorial comments, opinions, or judgments are to be included. The children can exchange papers to check for accuracy in the biographies.

### 8. Reference

Reichard, Cary L., and Blackburn, Dennis B. 1973, pp. 191–92. This book suggests a number of songs with related activities for developing writing.

## Art Experiences and Related Games, Crafts, and Projects

### 1. Creative Thinking

Materials: Such common objects as boxes, packing materials, rocks, shells, rope; drawing paper; paints.

Procedure: Display the materials and discuss the function, use, and purpose of each. Then have each child select one object and perceive a way to use it in a manner different from its original intent. A rock could be a doorstop; a rope could be used as a swing. Each child then draws and paints a picture to illustrate the use of the object in a different way. The drawings are shared, and other children suggest additional uses for the object and expand on the use suggested by the first child. Each child then writes a creative composition based on the new use or uses or pretends to be the item and writes a first-person account of how it feels to function in this way.

### 2. Creative Thinking

Materials: Drawing paper, paints, crayons.

Procedure: Each person selects an interesting odor. Working with color, each child creates a picture story expressing the feelings or actions suggested by the odor. Following a discussion of the pictures, each child writes a story about the odor. When the children have learned to do this well, the activity can be expanded to include several odors at once using more than one art medium to express the feelings evoked by the odor (King, 1975, p. 246).

### 3. Creative Thinking

Materials: Large sheets of manila paper, crayons, masking tape.

Procedure: Give each child a large piece of manila paper that has been folded in half. A manila folder can be used also. The front half of the folder is cut into three or four strips, as shown in figure 2–2. The first child closes the folder and opens only the top section, where the child then draws a head of any kind. The top section is taped closed and the folder is passed to the next child, who opens the second section and draws a neck and the top of a torso of any kind. That section is then taped closed and the folder is passed to a third child, who opens the third section and draws the waist to the knees. After the section is taped closed, the folder is passed to the last child, who opens the fourth section and draws the knees to the feet. If only three sections are used, the three parts would be head and neck, body and arms, and legs and feet.

The completed picture is passed to the next child, who opens it up and uses it to write creatively using one of the following activities:

a. Name the creature and tell where it came from.
b. Write a poem about the creature.
c. Create a story with the creature in it.
d. Write a play about the creature.
e. Write about the personal traits and characteristics of the creature.
f. Create a language for the creature. Make up words the creature might use in its homeland. Spell them phonetically.
g. Write a short story telling what the creature would do if it were in the situation described on the situation card given to you.

**Figure 2-2**

This activity can be adapted to the social studies program by having the children create drawings related to particular time periods or countries (Smith, 1974).

## 4. CREATIVE THINKING

MATERIALS: Thought-provoking drawings, photos, paintings, or pieces of artwork.

PROCEDURE: Display a number of artworks as a stimulus for writing. Self-created modernistic works using paint blots can also be used effectively. The children are asked to look at all the works carefully, to note what thoughts come to mind, and to write a story that includes all the works displayed. The children can illustrate the finished stories. In addition, since the same stimulus was used for everyone, it is interesting to have the children compare and contrast their stories.

## 5. CREATIVE THINKING

MATERIALS: Drawing paper, crayons, paints.

PROCEDURE: Have the students draw and color or paint a picture emphasizing a repetition of color sequences. Establish a color–musical note relationship, for example, green = middle "c," blue = "d." Then, working from left to right, have the children convert the color sequences in their pictures into notes. The notes are then played or sung by the student or the teacher to make a melody. The students make up words for their own songs or write stories for their songs. In some cases, a particular melody may be so nice that the students may decide that they prefer to write words to that one rather than their own.

## 6. INTERPRETING SENSORY PERCEPTIONS

MATERIALS: Drawing paper, crayons, paint, recorded instrumental music.

PROCEDURE: The children are instructed to draw or paint to recreate a mood or image received while listening to music. The children should listen to the recording first and not attempt to draw until the second playing. They can be given a completely free hand in the creation of their pictures or they can be instructed to draw "to" the music, that is, to use short lines for fast movements and long lines for slow ones. Different kinds of reproductions can be assigned for loud and soft tones, high and low tones, and so forth. When the pictures are finished, the children write creatively to express what they felt.

## 7. SEQUENCING ACTION

MATERIALS: Tag board 3 inches x 16 inches, crayons, scissors, magazines, glue.

PROCEDURE: Each student decides on a theme or a subject for a story. Each looks through magazines for pictures to illustrate the story. The tagboard is folded like an accordion, and one picture is pasted onto each panel. Each child then writes a story to accompany the pictures (Taylor et al., 1970, task 77).

## 8. RESEARCH AND WRITING

MATERIALS: Large sheets of drawing paper, crayons, paint.

PROCEDURE: Have each child select a particular month of the year, being certain that each month has been chosen at least once. Each child then researches which painters, architects, and sculptors were born in the month selected. The children then create calendars, with illustrations, for their months and fill in the particular dates on which the births occurred. When the calendars are completed, each child writes about the month researched. Finally, the twelve months are shared in discussion.

## 9. WRITING FACTUALLY

MATERIALS: Biographies of the lives of painters, architects, sculptors.

PROCEDURE: Follow the same procedure as described in experience 7 in the section on music experiences.

## 10. FOSTERING CREATIVITY

MATERIALS: Illustrated advertisements.

PROCEDURE: Have the children write or rewrite the text for product advertisements using the illustrations as a guide and as a springboard for ideas.

## 11. FOSTERING CREATIVITY

MATERIALS: Camera, film, cardboard, shoeboxes.

PROCEDURE: A number of photographic projects can be used in the classroom. Waller (1981) describes quite a few to facilitate learner interaction and participation.

a. The students make a photo album by cutting the cover and the inside pages into a particular shape such as a dog, pitcher, or house. Photos are mounted on each page to illustrate a story. Captions are written.
b. Students write original stories and put them into book form. The stories are illustrated with the students' photographs.
c. A photograph is glued to a piece of cardboard or construction paper, and a long slit is cut in the cardboard under the photo. The students write stories about the picture. The story is pulled down through the slit in the cardboard to be read.
d. The students write autobiographies or biographies and illustrate them with photographs of the people involved.

## 12. Expressing Feelings*

MATERIALS: A light source, large white drawing paper, colored construction paper, glue, magazines, scissors, pencils.

PROCEDURE: One at a time, a light source is shone toward a child who is standing against a surface, such as the wall, with white paper tacked to it. As the child's profile is silhouetted, another child outlines the profile with a pencil. The finished silhouette is cut out and glued to a piece of colored construction paper. When all the silhouettes are ready, the children are given a variety of magazines. They are asked to think about what they are like; their feelings, dreams, and desires. They are then to cut from the magazines pictures that represent their inner selves, and paste them inside the profile.

The finished products are shared and discussed, compared and contrasted. The children are led to see how each person is unique and special.

Children could also be asked to represent a specific thing in the profiles, such as the saddest day of their lives, what they would like to be like in the future, and so forth.

*Contributed by Christy Ocskay, Reno, Nevada.

## 13. Reference

DONHAM, JEAN, AND ICKEN, MARY (1977). Twenty-five picture books are discussed. Related art activities that can be used with them are suggested. The artwork in picture books and in children's literature can serve as a natural stimulus for writing.

# Drama Experiences and Related Games, Crafts, and Projects

## 1. INTERPRETING SOUNDS

MATERIALS: Nothing special required.

PROCEDURE: Have each child experiment with making sounds in different ways: hitting the thigh with the hand, striking glasses filled with water. Begin by working in pairs; one child makes the sound and the other listens with eyes closed. The child who is listening tells what image came to mind, what might come next. The roles are then reversed. The children use the sound and the images to write a story. The important thing to focus on is not what made the sound but the thoughts that came to mind on hearing it (King, 1975, pp. 223, 224).

## 2. INTERPRETING SOUNDS

MATERIALS: Nothing special required.

PROCEDURE: Instruct each child in the group to select a sound and then make that sound for the others. After hearing all the sounds, each child writes a story by putting the sounds together as if they were words. Each of the sounds must be discussed before the writing (King, 1975, p. 247).

## 3. EXPRESSING MOOD

MATERIALS: Recorded music of varying tempos.

PROCEDURE: Play music that suggests such different movements as hopping, running, galloping, skipping, jumping, or such different feelings as happiness and sadness. After listening once, the children move to the music, as it is played again, in the manner it suggests to them. They then write a composition about what the music made them think of.

## 4. DEVELOPING CHARACTERIZATION

MATERIALS: Construction paper, paint, crayons, glue, string, yarn, and other items to decorate a mask.

PROCEDURE: Have the children create a three-dimensional mask, put it on, and assume a body position that corresponds to the mask. A discussion should then ensue on how the character would feel, think, and act. The children exchange masks and discuss a variety of interpretations of the character. The children then paint pictures to show how the character makes them feel, where it lives, what it does, and so forth. Using the painting as a base, the children write a story about the character. This activity can be incorporated with the social studies program by establishing a different time period or country for the character (King, 1975, pp. 202, 203).

### 5. CREATIVE THINKING

MATERIALS: Nothing special required.

PROCEDURE: A child is given a situation, with a series of actions, to pantomime. The situation could be riding on a bus, going to the doctor, shopping in the supermarket, and so forth. The other children watch the pantomime, decide what is being acted out, and write a story about it. The stories are read aloud, compared, and contrasted. A discussion should ensue on why different interpretations were evident.

## GRAMMAR

The experiences in this area include materials for teaching and practicing sentence types, comparative words, verb forms, and parts of speech.

## Music Experiences and Related Games, Crafts, and Projects

### 1. RECOGNIZING SENTENCE TYPES

MATERIALS: A number of different kinds of simple musical instruments.

PROCEDURE: Hand out three types of instruments, such as drums, castanets, and harmonicas or xylophones. Each instrument is designated to represent a different type of sentence; that is, the drum can be a declarative sentence, which needs a period at the end; the castanets can be an interrogative sentence, which needs a question mark, and so forth. One child is selected as the leader and prepares a number of different sentences. The child reads each sentence aloud, one at a time, and everyone holding the instrument representing that type of sentence plays a sound on the instrument. In some instances, it may be best for the teacher to prepare the sentences (Nash et al., 1977, p. 102). This activity can be expanded to complex and compound sentences and to such other aspects of grammar as parts of speech and punctuation marks.

## 2. Recognizing Parts of Speech

MATERIALS: A recording of a popular song known by the children, copies of the lyrics for each of the children, crayons.

PROCEDURE: Play the recording for the children. Then hand out the copies of the lyrics. Explain that the song will be played over again a few times and that, while it is being played, the children are to draw crayon marks through the words as follows: nouns in blue, verbs in green, adjectives in red, and so forth. The music is played until each of the children finishes the game and has marked as many words as can be found for each category. The children then count how many nouns, verbs, and so forth, they found, and a comparison is made. The child with the most correct responses in a given category can be awarded a prize or declared the winner. This activity is a variation on an experimental program being used in Austin, Texas. The program is called "Color Sounds" and was written by Mike Bell for Multimedia Learning Systems. Its intent is to provide phonics practice. The experimental program is described in chapter 3, "Reading Experiences," in the section dealing with word recognition.

# Art Experiences and Related Games, Crafts, and Projects

## 1. Using Comparisons

MATERIALS: Nothing special required.

PROCEDURE: Give a group of children a position word of comparison. The group must then create a picture to represent the word. The remaining children try to figure out the word from the picture. Teamwork can be established by presenting points and determining a winning team.

## 2. Recognizing Verb Forms

MATERIALS: A variety of pictures representing things in the past, things in the present, and things in the future.

PROCEDURE: Give three pictures to each child, one representing the past, one the present, and one the future. Or, one third of the group can be given each type of picture. One child is selected to make up and read a list of verbs. It may be necessary for the teacher to compile the list. The child reads the list of verbs word one at a time. The children holding the picture that corresponds with the tense of the verb holds it up. Or, if each child has three pictures, each one selects the picture to hold up which illustrates the tense of the verb. This activity can be expanded to more complex verb tense forms.

### 3. Using Descriptive Language*

MATERIALS: A colorful picture.

PROCEDURE: Display the picture for the children. Suggest that this is a game to find out about the things in the picture. Name an item. Then ask the children to think of words that "tell about" or describe the objects named. If a cat was pictured and that word was called, the children could say, "a sleepy cat," "a yellow cat," and so forth. The children are encouraged to describe the object with as many different words as possible. All the words and phrases are written on the board. These can then be used to build sentences and stories. For students who can work independently, each can be given a picture and asked to list all the descriptive words and phrases that come to mind as a result of viewing the picture. The children's thinking should be directed so that they include adverbs and adjectives.

*Contributed by Claudette Donnelly, Saunderstown, R. I.

### 4. Using Descriptive Language*

MATERIALS: Three colors of finger paint, 12-inch × 18-inch finger paint paper, 12-inch × 18-inch white paper, newspaper, small dishes of water, crayons, felt-tip pens.

PROCEDURE: As a starting point for learning descriptive adjectives and adverbs, the children will make monoprints. The steps are (a) Cover the table with newspaper. (b) Put the finger paint paper on the newspaper and then, using different motions with the fingers and arms, cover the paper with paint. (c) Take the white paper and press it onto the covered painted paper. When the white paper is lifted, the transferred painting is the accomplished monoprint. (d) After the monoprint is dry, add to it with crayons or felt-tip pens.

The students are asked if their finished pictures look like anything. Have the students turn their pictures sideways and upside down to get different views and different ideas. Ask what feelings the picture evokes. Does it make them feel sad, worried, happy? Elicit words that describe the way the painting looks and how the students feel. Write the words on the board. Lead the students to see that these words are adjectives and adverbs and to recognize their characteristics. Then have the children write a few sentences about what their picture looks like using as many adjectives and adverbs as possible.

*Contributed by Beverly Harrison, East Greenwich, R. I.

### 5. USING DESCRIPTIVE LANGUAGE*

MATERIALS: Drawing paper and crayons.
PROCEDURE: Discuss the meaning of metaphor and provide many examples. The children then select metaphorical phrases and draw literal illustrations of them. Examples of phrases which might be used include: a taste of defeat, the sweet smell of success, getting to the heart of the matter, a babbling brook, time flies, and a blanket of snow.

The pictures are apt to be funny and humorous. Since they deal with absurdities, the children are not as likely to have preconceived notions of how their renditions should look. The finished illustrations should be shared with the class. The rest of the group can attempt to guess which metaphor was illustrated.

Discussion should follow on how metaphors are used to expand meaning from something we know to something new and on the relationship between the literal and metaphorical meaning of the words. The children can look for metaphors in written works and can write original material containing metaphors.

*Contributed by Susanne Shindler, Incline Village, Nevada.

## Drama Experiences and Related Games, Crafts, and Projects

### 1. USING COMPARISONS

MATERIALS: Nothing special required.
PROCEDURE: The children are divided into groups of three. Each group is given a position word of comparison: small, smaller, smallest; big, bigger, biggest. The groups take time to plan how they will act out their words using movement. When ready, the groups present their words for the others to figure out by asking questions and making guesses. Points can be given to the group for each question that must be asked or for each incorrect guess before the correct answer is determined. The group with the fewest points is the winner (Nash et al., 1977, p. 99).

## 2. Using Verbs and Adverbs

MATERIALS: Nothing special required.

PROCEDURE: Present verbs and adverbs to the students. Instruct them to move as the words direct, for example, run slowly, tap gently. This can be played as a game. The words can be presented to the students secretly. Other pupils or groups can then attempt to determine what is being acted out.

# SPELLING

The spelling experiences include identifying homonyms, recognizing words, reinforcing difficult words, and practicing spelling words.

## Music Experiences and Related Games, Crafts, and Projects

### 1. Identifying Homonyms

MATERIALS: Nothing special required.

PROCEDURE: The teacher sings the letters of a word that has a homonym by going up the scale, for example, b-l-u-e. The child responds by singing the letters of the homonym by going down the scale: b-l-e-w. The child starts at the note where the teacher left off. In that way, the child is repeating the scale the teacher sang but in reverse. Or, the child may spell the new word by going up the scale, continuing where the teacher left off. When the homonym is longer than the original word, the child continues going down (or up) the scale and when the next word is presented, the teacher begins again where the child left off (Nash, et al., 1977, p. 104).

### 2. Spelling Musically*

MATERIALS: Copies of a musical staff.

PROCEDURE: The children are taught the names of the musical notes and their positions on the staff. The five lines are E G B D F and the four spaces are F A C E . The children are asked to write down as many words as they can think of which use only the letters on the staff. They should be given a sufficient amount of time to do this. They are then asked to plot their words on the staff paper, placing one word to each bar. (See figure 2–3.) The children exchange papers and try to figure out the other student's words by reading the notes and converting them to letters.

*Contributed by Nora Safford, Charlestown, R. I.

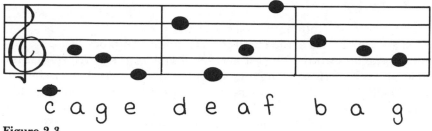

**Figure 2-3**

### 3. Recognizing Words*

Materials: A music maze.
Procedure: Give the children a music maze puzzle.

MUSIC MAZE
*How many music words can you find? You might find the words going across or going down. After you circle the word, write it on a line down the side of the paper.*

A F J S B I D H K H U M_____
D Z S O N G G D C A E E_____
I M I F A P E T O N E L_____
C O N T A O S D F B U O_____
T B G R C O K I A Q S D_____
S A O A E N L U S A S Y_____
O Y O S X L I S T E N S_____
L O U D U P B W B X O S_____
O G E N O T E S L M Y K_____
R U E E R E A V E T A O_____
Y S L O W X T O T O R O_____
O A T J E K M Z I L C B_____

For younger children, the words should be listed on the side of the paper and the word found, circled, and rewritten. This maze can be constructed using vocabulary from art, drama, social studies, or science.

*Contributed by Claudette Donnelly, Saunderstown, R. I.

### 4. Reinforcing Difficult Words

Materials: A list of difficult spelling words in which one or more letters have been left out of each word.
Procedure: Once the children have learned the musical notes of the scale, the list of difficult spelling words is presented. The children must apply the missing letters from those of the musical scale, for example, s–p–r–te.

### 5. Spelling Musically*

MATERIALS: Nothing special required.

PROCEDURE: Have the children determine a number of 3-, 4-, and 5-letter spelling words. The list may be placed on the board so that the children can sing the spelling song moving from one word to another, or individual children may each add a verse as the song moves from one child to another.

Using the melody "Farmer in the Dell" the children would sing, for the word "happy," "We're h-a-p-p-y. We're h-a-p-p-y. We know we are, we're sure we are, we're h-a-p-p-y."

With three-letter words they would sing, "We're s-a-d. We're sad," etc. With four-letter words they would sing, "We're g-l-a-d glad," etc.

*Contributed by Thomas J. Montague, M.Ed., Reno, Nevada.

## Art Experiences and Related Games, Crafts, and Projects

### 1. Drawing Words

MATERIALS: Art paper and pencils.

PROCEDURE: To practice the spelling of difficult concrete words, have the children create a picture using the word or words they are having trouble mastering. One or more completed pictures should be shown to the children as examples so that they understand what they are to do. (See figure 2–4.)

**Figure 2-4**

## 2. DICTIONARY MAKING

MATERIALS: Drawing paper, crayons, paints.
PROCEDURE: Have the children construct a picture dictionary. All words should be illustrated, and definitions should be included. This activity can be related to specific content areas. A science illustrated dictionary can be made, or one for social studies, and so forth.

## 3. REINFORCING DIFFICULT WORDS

MATERIALS: Drawing paper, crayons.
PROCEDURE: Have the children make word rebuses for difficult spelling words. When no picture can be drawn or cut from a magazine or newspaper to represent a letter, the letter is written in. A game can be played in which the children exchange rebuses. Each child then tries to determine what word the other child was portraying. It is important that the children be shown a number of examples so they understand the concept of the rebus. (See figure 2–5.)

**Figure 2-5**

## 4. EXPANDING SPELLING ABILITY

MATERIALS: Drawing paper, crayons or paint.
PROCEDURE: Select a place or thing and have the children draw a picture of it and paint or crayon the finished product. The place or thing selected should present the opportunity for artistic work. "Battle" is one word that could be used. The children turn the paper over and write the word on the back of the picture. They then make as many words as possible from the letters of the word illustrated. If "battle" was the word, they could list, for example, "bat," "let," "tab," "lab," "bale." This activity can be related to the science or social studies programs by using words related to the area under study.

## 5. REINFORCING DIFFICULT WORDS

MATERIALS: Drawing paper and crayon.
PROCEDURE: Have the children draw a picture of a difficult spelling word to be learned. Each child should have a different word. When the children complete the pictures, they are instructed to write a sentence

using the letters of the illustrated word as the initial letter of each word in the sentence, for example, "nation" = "Ned and Ted insist on neatness," "latitude" = "Let's all talk in turn until day ends." The children can exchange sentences and try to figure out the spelling word from the sentence. When the game is finished, each child's picture is labeled with the sentence. A bulletin board of pictures, words, and sentences can be set up.

### 6. DISGUISING WORDS

MATERIALS: Drawing paper, crayons, paints.

PROCEDURE: The children are instructed to draw a picture and to hide the letters of a word in it. They should add things to the picture so that the letters are harder to find. The children exchange pictures and try to find the hidden word or words. When they find them they write them down. At a given signal, the children exchange papers again, with someone else, and find the hidden word(s) in the new picture. This continues until each child has seen all the pictures drawn by every other child. The child who has spotted the most words correctly is the winner. (See figure 2–6.)

Figure 2-6

## Drama Experiences and Related Games, Crafts, and Projects

### 1. SPELLING CHARADE

MATERIALS: Nothing special required.

PROCEDURE: Two teams, of equal number, are formed. Each team determines a list of action words, one word for each child on the team. The first member of one team spells a word for the first member of the other team. The child listening must figure out the word and show that the word is known by doing the appropriate action, for example, g–r–i–n, c–l–a–p, f–r–o–w–n. If the child does the action correctly, that team gets a point. If the child misses, the point is given to the team spelling the word. The game continues by alternating from one team to the other, as in a spelling bee, until each child has had a turn at giving a spelling word and acting one out.

## 2. REINFORCING DIFFICULT WORDS

MATERIALS: Nothing special required.
PROCEDURE: Compile a list of new and troublesome spelling words. The children are instructed to write a story using all the words in the list. Each story is read aloud. One is then chosen by the students to be dramatized.

# REFERENCES

DONHAM, JEAN, AND ICKEN, MARY. "Reading to Write: An Approach to Composition Using Picture Books." *Language Arts* 54 (May 1977): 555–58.

KING, NANCY. *Giving Form to Feeling.* New York: Drama Book Specialists/Publishers, 1975.

NASH, GRACE C.; JONES, GERALDINE W.; POTTER, BARBARA A.; AND SMITH, PATSY F. *The Child's Way of Learning.* Sherman Oaks, Calif.: Alfred Publishing Co., 1977.

REICHARD, CARY L., AND BLACKBURN, DENNIS B. *Music Based Instruction for the Exceptional Child.* Denver: Love Publishing Co., 1973.

SMITH, JAMES A. *Adventures in Communication.* Boston: Allyn and Bacon, 1974.

TAYLOR, FRANK D., ARTUSO, ALFRED A., AND HEWETT, FRANK M. *Creative Art Tasks for Children.* Denver: Love Publishing Co., 1970.

WALLER, VICTORIA MILLER. "Lights, Camera, Action! The Camera as a Tool for Teaching Reading." In *Motivating Reluctant Readers,* edited by Alfred J. Ciani. Newark, Del.: International Reading Association, 1981, pp. 90–97.

# CHAPTER 3

# Reading Experiences

THE EXPERIENCES IN THIS CHAPTER are presented in six broad skill areas: word recognition, comprehension, study skills, stimulating reading, processing, and vocabulary. Each of the areas of music, art, and drama are not equally applicable to every skill area.

## WORD RECOGNITION

The activities in this section are designed to provide practice in and teaching materials for the following skills: the alphabet, phonics, prefixes and suffixes, and syllabication.

### Music Experiences and Related Games, Crafts, and Projects

1. ESTABLISHING LETTER RELATIONSHIPS

MATERIALS: Nothing special required.

PROCEDURE: Teach the children a number of alphabet songs. Many children's and adult songs can be used to foster the learning of the alphabet, including "A You're Adorable" and the ever-popular songs from the *Sound of Music*. After teaching a few songs, encourage the children to make up their own lyrics to an alphabet song. They can use any of the melodies previously learned.

## 2. HEARING SOUNDS

MATERIALS: A recording of a popular song, multiple copies of the lyrics of the song, crayons.

PROCEDURE: This activity, called "Color Sounds," was written by Mike Bell and is produced by Multimedia Learning Systems. It is being used experimentally in Austin, Texas. Each of the sixteen vowel sounds is assigned a color. A popular song is played, and the children mark the words of the song with the correct color representing the sound. A different song is used each week. The children try to see how many instances of a particular sound they can find and mark and whether they are able to find all examples of a particular sound. For each song, all sixteen vowel sounds are being sought.

## 3. RECOGNIZING WORD PARTS

MATERIALS: A list of musical words containing prefixes and suffixes.

PROCEDURE: Have the children identify prefixes and suffixes in musical words, discuss the meanings of the elements in relation to the meaning of the words, and compare the meanings of the elements with their use in nonmusical words.

Suffixes that can be used include "-issimo" (pianissimo), "-ino" (andantino), "-tion" and "-ation" (improvisation), "-etto" (allegretto), and "-do" (accelerando).

Prefixes that can be found include "de-" (decrescendo), "semi-" (semicadence), "en-" (enharmonic), "sub-" (subdominant), "dis-" (dissonance), and "mono-" (monophonic).

## 4. RHYMING WORDS

MATERIALS: An instrumental recording with a four-quarter beat.

PROCEDURE: Play the recording. Have the children clap to the beat after the way to do this has been demonstrated. Explain that this is a game. The first person is to call out a word. Then everyone will clap to the four beats. On the fourth beat, the next person will name a new word that rhymes with the first one. This is continued until someone cannot think of a word or repeats a word. The person who misses then thinks of a new word to start the game again (Reichard and Blackburn, 1973, p. 57.)

## 5. Hearing Beat

MATERIALS: A number of rhythm instruments, a well-known song written in four-quarter time, with lyrics.

PROCEDURE: Write out the song in simple form, such as is shown in figure 3–1. Give the children rhythm instruments and instruct them to shake or hit the instrument on each beat. If no instruments are available, they can clap their hands. Have the children note that the longer words, the words with more than one part, get more than one beat. Let them suggest other songs and beat them out in like manner. They may sing along as they tap out the rhythm. It is advantageous for the children to see the words as they are doing this. In this way they can build an association between the auditory and the visual.

Yan - kee  Doo - dle  went  to  Lon - don  rid - ing  on  a    etc.

**Figure 3-1**

## 6. Hearing Beat

MATERIALS: Nothing special required.

PROCEDURE: Have children clap the rhythm of individual words, words in songs, and names. They can also be asked to note the accented syllables in words that are sung. A game can be played. The children sit in a circle. The first child calls out the name of the child to the right while clapping the proper number of beats. The next child calls out the name of the next child to the right, and claps the beats. This continues until everyone has had a chance. The circle can begin again by using the last names. The teacher can liven up the game by changing the directions in midstream, which is a good way to develop listening skills too.

## 7. Recognizing Phonic Elements*

MATERIALS: Recorded music, a chair for each child in the group, word cards representing a specific phonic element, flash cards of the phonic elements.

PROCEDURE: This game is played like Musical Chairs. It can be played using initial, medial, or final sounds and long or short vowels. It can also be used for vocabulary development by using homonyms, synonyms, or antonyms. Flash cards of words containing the phonic element to be reinforced are taped onto the chairs. If long vowels were being practiced, the word taped on each chair would contain a long vowel sound. Each child is then given a flash card with one of the long vowel sounds on it. The music is turned on and the children march around the chairs. When the music stops, each child sits down on the nearest chair. Then each child checks the flash card with the word on the chair. If the sound matches, the child remains seated. If not, the game continues with the children who have not yet found a match. The game continues until all the chairs have been taken.

*Contributed by Maureen Harrington, Westerly, R.I.

## 8. References

Palmer, Hap. #AR514 and AR522. Music activities for the alphabet and for consonants are included. In "Marching Around the Alphabet," the letters of the alphabet are placed in a circle on the floor. The children march around and, when the music stops, they select a letter closest to their feet. When they are called on, they say the letter. The game continues so that the children get different letters to call. The game can also be played like Musical Chairs, wherein one child is eliminated at each round. In "Something That Begins Like," pictures of objects are displayed. Upon directions from the music, the children locate the pictures beginning with the particular sound named in the song.

# Art Experiences and Related Games, Crafts, and Projects

## 1. Using Sounds

Materials: Nothing special required.
Procedure: Play a game in which the first child gives a phonic element, such as long "a," and the other children must name something related to art which has that sound. The children can go in order. When a child misses, a point is given and that child names a different phonic element to continue the game. The child with the fewest points is the winner. Examples of words that might be used include "paint," "paper," and "clay."

## 2. Understanding Prefixes

Materials: Drawing paper, paint, crayons.
Procedure: Have the children create pictures to represent prefix meanings, for example, a picture of something depressed, a picture of something inverted. If the children themselves are unable to think of

examples, a list of suggestions may have to be given to them. The finished pictures are exhibited, and the other children try to determine what is pictured and what prefix is being portrayed. A number of pictures illustrating the same prefix can be contrasted and compared.

### 3. Establishing Letter Relationships

MATERIALS: Drawing paper, paint, crayons.
PROCEDURE: Have the children make their own alphabet books, illustrating each letter. Plenty of room should be left so that the children can add drawings of additional things they think of or pictures of items they find.

### 4. Learning Letters

MATERIALS: Drawing paper, crayons, paints.
PROCEDURE: Have the children design a picture for each letter of the alphabet which will include the letter itself, for example, a flower's stem and bottom two leaves could become an "r." Encourage creativity on the part of the children and have them observe common objects closely to see if they can see a letter in them. The children should not be asked to complete the entire alphabet in one sitting. This activity should continue over a period of time, allowing the children ample opportunity to observe objects and think of new ones.

### 5. Using Sounds

MATERIALS: Drawing paper, crayons, paint.
PROCEDURE: Have the children make an illustrated phonics dictionary. The same procedures should be followed as described in making an alphabet book, experience 3.

### 6. Hearing Syllables

MATERIALS: A list of words used in art.
PROCEDURE: Present a list of such common terms used in art as "paint," "brushes," "easel," and "paper." For each word, the children clap out the syllables. This can be played in game form. Have the children sit in a circle. The first child thinks of an art term and tells how many syllables are in it, the second child thinks of another term and gives the number of syllables, and so forth. When a child misses, a point is given and the game continues with the next child. The one with the fewest points is the winner. The game can be played using the names of painters, sculptors,

or architects. When the children are required to think of their own words, the game is more valuable in respect to achieving both word recognition and art objectives.

### 7. ILLUSTRATING SYLLABLES

MATERIALS: Drawing paper, crayons, paint.
PROCEDURE: Each child selects a noun and then must draw a picture of it so that the picture of the word is divided into the number of syllables in the word. An automobile, for example, could be drawn showing four distinct parts: the engine, the front seat, the back seat, the trunk.

### 8. REFERENCE

The Acorn is a quarterly newspaper publication for teachers that includes many creative activities and games for various reading skills, mathematics, science, and social studies. It is published by Bur Oak Press, Inc., Route 3, Box 193, Platteville, WI. 53818.

## Drama Experiences and Related Games, Crafts, and Projects

### 1. UNDERSTANDING PREFIXES AND SUFFIXES

MATERIALS: A list of words that can be affixed.
PROCEDURE: Give each child a word without an affix and then with the prefix or suffix added. Each child must then act out the word to show the change as a result of the addition of the affix. The other children attempt to figure out the two words being depicted. This can be played as a game with points awarded for correct responses.

### 2. USING INITIAL CONSONANTS

MATERIALS: Nothing special required.
PROCEDURE: Teach the chant:

Tell us please
If you can
What word starts
Just like —.

Any rhyming word can be used, such as "man," "ban," "Dan," "fan," "pan," "Nan." The rhyme can be adjusted, and the chant can be extended to final sounds as well as vowels.

The children chant and clap the rhythm. Each child in turn responds while clapping:

Child 1      [Clap, clap, clap,]
             I'll say "milk"

Child 2      [Clap, clap, clap,]
             I'll say "march"

# COMPREHENSION

This section contains experiences for cause-and-effect relationships, concept development, critical thinking, and details and main ideas.

## Music Experiences and Related Games, Crafts, and Projects

### 1. CHANGING MOODS

MATERIALS: Recorded music evoking different moods.

PROCEDURE: Discuss how things may happen as a result of something else. Give the children the opportunity to provide many examples. Talk about why something happens after a particular thing. Explain, and lead the children to generalize, that we often feel a certain way because of how something else acts upon us. Demonstrate by first getting the children to laugh and then immediately playing some music that will evoke the feeling of sadness. Ask the children how they now feel and why. Then play music that makes the children think of happy things. Lead the children to see how their moods have changed. Encourage the children to find music that makes them feel a particular way and to determine what it is about the music that makes them feel that way. Lead them into a recognition of cause-and-effect relationships. Also, have them examine music in which feelings change within the one piece and examine how the music did this.

### 2. APPRECIATING MUSICAL ACCOMPANIMENT

MATERIALS: A television set.

PROCEDURE: Have the children watch a particular television show. If there is no set available for the classroom, the children can be assigned to do the viewing at home. It is best, however, if they can all watch at the same time. Discuss what feelings the music in the program evoked, how the music related to the story, the differences that might occur if different music were played or if there were no music. The children must be directed to think critically about the relationship between the music and the story.

## 3. Selecting Music Critically

MATERIALS:  Nothing special required.

PROCEDURE:  As an assignment to do at home, have the children prepare a story to read aloud and select music to play as a background for the reading. The musical selections should enhance the story in some way. After the story is read with the musical background, have the children discuss what the music made the listeners think of and whether the music helped to develop the mood or theme of the story or the characterizations. As the children become more proficient, let them select a number of musical pieces to play during the reading so that the mood can be adjusted to fit the story.

## 3. Analyzing Music Critically

MATERIALS:  A recording of classical music.

PROCEDURE:  Play a piece of classical music. Discuss how the composer might have felt when writing the music, what feelings the composer wanted to arouse, what the composer might have been writing about. Discuss what elements of the music produced the feeling and mood.

## 4. Recognizing Mood

MATERIALS:  Several pictures and several pieces of music related to the pictures.

PROCEDURE:  Show the children several pictures depicting moods or actions, such as sadness, jumping, swimming. Display the pictures and discuss the moods or actions of each. Then play music that associates with the mood or action of each picture, and ask the children to determine to which picture each musical composition relates. Discuss why a particular picture was chosen and why another picture was not. Then remove the pictures and replay the songs. The children must then describe from memory the picture that relates to each song (Reichard and Blackburn, 1973, p. 63).

## 5. Listening Critically for Main Idea

MATERIALS:  An instrumental recording.

PROCEDURE:  Play an instrumental musical recording. Have the children determine a title for it by taking the mood and feeling into consideration. Then compare their titles with the original title and discuss the differences and why they occurred.

## 6. Using Details

MATERIALS: Copies of song lyrics.
PROCEDURE: Give the children the lyrics to a song they do not know. Have them determine a title for the song based upon the lyrics. Compare their results with the original title and discuss the differences found.

## 7. Using Main Idea

MATERIALS: A song title.
PROCEDURE: Give the children the title to a song they do not know. Have them write lyrics to fit the title. Then compare their lyrics with the original. Discuss which are better and why, and how the children's lyrics differed from the original, and why.

## 8. Developing Concepts

MATERIALS: Nothing special required.
PROCEDURE: Teach the well-known song "Round and Round the Village." Then have the children form a single circle with hands joined. One student is selected to be on the outside of the circle. The following words are sung as the circle moves to the right. The person outside the circle walks in the opposite direction.

> Go round and round the village
> Go round and round the village
> Go round and round the village
> As we have done before.

At this point everyone stops, and the joined hands are raised forming "windows." As the group continues to sing, the player on the outside goes in and out under the raised arms, ending up in the center of the circle.

> Go in and out the window
> Go in and out the window
> Go in and out the window
> As we have done before.

The children continue to sing, and the player in the center now chooses a partner and stands in front of the student chosen.

> Now stand and face your partner
> Now stand and face your partner

Now stand and face your partner
As we have done before.

As the final chorus is sung, the player and the partner selected skip around the outside of the circle.

Now follow me to London [or any other city selected]
Now follow me to London
Now follow me to London
As we have done before.

The sequence is continued with the player and the partner on the outside of the circle. The game is continued until everyone has been chosen. If the group is very large, begin the game with two players on the outside.

## 9. REFERENCE

PALMER, HAP. #AR522. Development of the concept of body parts can be assisted by one of Palmer's activities. He includes a song, "Let's Dance," in which the body parts of front, back, and side are identified while the children follow the directions of the song.

# Art Experiences and Related Games, Crafts, and Projects

## 1. INTERPRETING EFFECTS

MATERIALS: A number of interesting photographs, drawings, or paintings.

PROCEDURE: The children are asked to look carefully at a picture or photo. They may work individually or in small groups. After viewing the picture or photo, each child writes five questions beginning, "What would happen if . . .?" Each question should have a realm of possibility: a new ending, a new character, and so forth. If several children are using the same picture or photo, have them prepare their questions separately. When everyone is ready, the children share their questions while the entire group views the original artwork and suggests answers to the questions as well as other questions. The emphasis is on "If this happens, then what else would have to happen?" (King, 1975, p. 174).

## 2. DEVELOPING CONCEPTS

MATERIALS: Drawing paper, crayons, paints.
PROCEDURE: After explaining the concept to be developed, (high-

low, up-down, big-small) have the children create pictures that demonstrate the concept. Once the children have learned a number of concepts, have each select one, create a picture to show it, and then exchange pictures to see if another child can figure out what concept is depicted.

### 3. Developing Concepts

MATERIALS: Drawing paper, crayons, paint.
PROCEDURE: Play a game in which individuals or teams must locate objects in the classroom, at home, or outdoors as examples of particular concepts to be developed. The students draw the objects. A book can be constructed with examples of things that are big and small, tall and short, and so forth.

### 4. Developing Concepts

MATERIALS: Drawing paper, crayons, paints.
PROCEDURE: Have the children create a picture based on the directions given. The directions should include the concepts to be reinforced, for example, "In your picture include a big tree and a small tree, more blue items than red items, an object going in and an object going out."

### 5. Recognizing Propaganda

MATERIALS: A number of advertisements.
PROCEDURE: Have the children analyze the pictures in advertisements to determine how the pictures attempt to sell the products. What feelings do the pictures arouse? In what ways do they make you feel you should buy the product? Are the pictures honest representations? Then have the children find their own advertisements in which the pictures are influential in selling the product. These are shared and discussed.

### 6. Understanding Perspective

MATERIALS: A number of photographs and pictures of the same ordinary objects.
PROCEDURE: Show the children two or more photos or pictures of the same object which were photographed, painted, or drawn from different perspectives. Lead the children, through discussion, to realize that things look different when approached from different angles. Extend this discussion into different points of view, issues, behaviors, and so forth. Have the children find photos and pictures that represent examples of different perspectives.

## 7. IMAGINING CRITICALLY

MATERIALS: Newspaper, picture of a magnified object.

PROCEDURE: Crumple a piece of newspaper and ask, "What shape could this be? What could it not be?" Show a picture of a common object magnified and ask the same questions. The purpose is to discover what is necessary and not necessary in identifying something. During the discussion, always ask why when the children suggest what an object could or could not be (King, 1975, p. 177).

## 8. RECOGNIZING PROPAGANDA

MATERIALS: A photograph from a newspaper story.

PROCEDURE: Give each child a copy of the photograph. Then instruct the children to crop the picture—cut it smaller—so the result gives a different story from the original. Discuss the different feelings and interpretations gleaned from the difference between the original and the cropped picture and why a newspaper photograph or one in a book might be cropped. The purpose is to get the children to realize that there are many different propaganda techniques and that they cannot always believe what they see.

## 9. READING PICTURES

MATERIALS: Illustrations from picture books, children's literature, or social studies books.

PROCEDURE: Show a picture to the children. After they study it carefully, ask a number of questions that can be answered by making inferences from things in the picture. A picture of an Indian village could provide information and clues to the kinds of homes the Indians lived in, what the homes were made of, whether they were permanent or portable, why they were permanent or portable, what the Indians ate, how they cooked, and so forth. The pictures can be used to develop the imagination, making of judgments, and critical thinking.

## 10. NOTING DETAILS

MATERIALS: A descriptive poem, drawing paper, crayons, paints.

PROCEDURE: Read a poem to the students. Instruct them to listen carefully in order to remember the details. After the reading, the children draw pictures to illustrate the poem, being certain to include as many details as possible. The finished products are compared and discussed and the poem is read again to check for accuracy.

## 11. Noting Details

MATERIALS: Clay.
PROCEDURE: Have the children make clay models of story characters including all the details they can. They can also make models of the settings, being certain to be accurate about the details. The finished products are displayed and discussed.

## 12. Noting Details

MATERIALS: Construction paper, drawing paper, crayons, paints.
PROCEDURE: All the following art activities can be used: making mobiles of characters or incidents, making dioramas of stories, making picture strips of plots, designing book jackets, and designing book posters.

## 13. Developing Understanding

MATERIALS: Comic Books.
PROCEDURE: Use comic books and cartoon making to teach key ideas, comprehension, and skimming. Children enjoy comic books, and the pictures provide the same opportunities as any other type of artwork (Sosnowski, 1975).

## 14. Demonstrating Comprehension

MATERIALS: Drawing paper, crayons, paints.
PROCEDURE: Have the children write and illustrate advertisements for books. To produce a good advertisement the child must have understood the story. This activity also reinforces vocabulary development.

## 15. Noting Details

MATERIALS: A number of series of pictures in which each picture in each series is similar in content.
PROCEDURE: Display a series of three pictures similar in content, such as pictures of a mother and child, people engaged in a sport, or a still life of a vase and flowers. Describe one of the pictures one detail at a time. After each detail is presented, discuss if the detail could apply to all three pictures, why it could, and why it could not. Keep adding details and discussing them until two of the pictures have been eliminated. Do this with a number of series of pictures, making the differentiations more difficult each time. Lead the children to see that they must have all the

details in order to determine the main idea. When they are able to handle this one detail at a time, read a number of details without discussing each individually, and then follow the same procedure.

## 16. NOTING DETAILS

MATERIALS: Pictures of various types of architecture.

PROCEDURE: Present pictures of buildings representing different architectural styles. Have the children note the differences and similarities in each of the different styles. Discuss which country or period each style represents. Then present a picture and have the children try to match the style to the country or to the period.

# Drama Experiences and Related Games, Crafts, and Projects

## 1. DEVELOPING CONCEPTS

MATERIALS: Large and small cardboard axes and large and small cardboard trees.

PROCEDURE: Give each child two cardboard axes, large and small, and two cardboard trees, large and small. Demonstrate the body movements of swinging an axe. Then, teach the song "Johnny Swings a Big Axe" and have the children sing along while another demonstration is given. The song is sung again and the children do the motions on their own. When the children are able to respond correctly, the activity is personalized by using the first names of the students instead of "Johnny" (Reichard and Blackburn, 1973, p. 35). (See figure 3–2.)

## 2. DEVELOPING CONCEPTS

MATERIALS: Nothing special required.

PROCEDURE: Have the children sing and act out such songs as "London Bridges," for the concepts of "up" and "down," and "Here We Go Looby Loo," for "in" and "out."

## 3. DEVELOPING CONCEPTS

MATERIALS: Nothing special required.

PROCEDURE: Use "up" and "down" in as many examples as possible. Be certain that each pupil understands the concept. Then teach the song

**Figure 3-2.** *(Reprinted from Cary L. Reichard and Dennis B. Blackburn, Music Based Instruction for The Exceptional Child, p. 35, with permission of Love Publishing Company, Denver, Colo.)*

"Bryan Jumps." While the students sing the song, it should be acted out for them. Following that, each student acts it out while the other pupils sing. The movement of "up" involves getting up on the toes with the arms stretched high. The "down" movement is accomplished by bending the knees down to the floor. The individual names of the students may be used instead of "Bryan" (Reichard and Blackburn, 1973, p. 37). (See figure 3–3.)

## Bryan Jumps

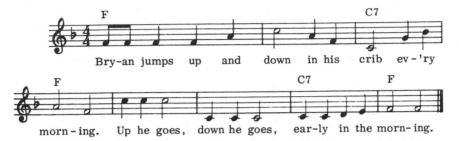

**Figure 3-3.** *(Reprinted from Cary L. Reichard and Dennis B. Blackburn, Music Based Instruction for The Exceptional Child, p. 37, with permission of Love Publishing Company, Denver, Colo.)*

### 4. DEVELOPING CONCEPTS

MATERIALS: Nothing special required.

PROCEDURE: Teach the following voice directions to develop the concepts of "high" and "low."

> soft to loud →
> whisper o
> voice getting higher ↑
> voice getting lower ↓

When the children understand the directions and are able to follow them, set up a dialogue in which the teacher speaks and the children answer.

> TEACHER   "Do you know what holiday is coming?" ↑
> STUDENTS  "Thanksgiving." o
> TEACHER   "When will it be?" ↑
> STUDENTS  "Next week." →
> TEACHER   "What will you eat?" ↑
> STUDENTS  "Turkey." o
> TEACHER   "And what else?" →
> STUDENTS  "Cranberry sauce." ↓

This activity can be extended by having the students accent the same way as the teacher, the opposite way, and by including body rhythms (Nash et al., 1977, p. 15).

### 5. Thinking Critically

MATERIALS: A film or television show of a ballet.

PROCEDURE: Have the children watch a ballet. Discuss how the movements of the dance fit with the music. Show the children how types of dance, such as the waltz, conform to the movements dictated by the music. Then play music and let the children determine the most appropriate movements.

### 6. Noting Main Ideas

MATERIALS: Puppet-making items.

PROCEDURE: Have the children make puppets of the characters from a particular story and then act out the story based on the main ideas.

## STUDY SKILLS

This section includes experiences for developing classification, categorization, and sequencing skills.

## Music Experiences and Related Games, Crafts, and Projects

### 1. Classifying Things

MATERIALS: Photographs, drawings, and paintings with many items displayed.

PROCEDURE: Teach the song "Bicycle Built for Two" using the following words:

> Daisy, Daisy look for the picture for me
> It will fit in, only this category
> We're looking for foods [cars, fruits, and so forth] aplenty
> Can you find one or twenty?
> Cause we'll have fun
> Till we are done
> Finding pictures of foods for me.

Display a picture. Start by using a child's name in place of "Daisy." If it is a one-syllable name sing, "Oh John, oh John." If the child called upon finds an item, then that child becomes the leader and sings the song to another child.

## 2. Recognizing Sequence

MATERIALS: Cut-up lyrics.
PROCEDURE: Teach songs that have a sequence, such as "Humpty Dumpty" and "Mary Had a Little Lamb." Put the lines of the lyrics on separate sheets of paper, mix them up, and have the children put them back together again in the correct sequence.

## 3. Using Sequence

MATERIALS: Nothing special required.
PROCEDURE: Have the children write new lyrics to a familiar tune in which they represent a sequence of actions. Discuss the lyrics to determine if they are in the correct order and if all the steps in the sequence have been included.

## 4. Establishing Sequence

MATERIALS: Nothing special required.
PROCEDURE: Older children may be asked to construct a time line of famous composers or performers or dancers. Research must be done first. The time lines would be compared and contrasted when finished.

# Art Experiences and Related Games, Crafts, and Projects

## 1. Classifying Things

MATERIALS: A picture containing many details.
PROCEDURE: Display the picture. Ask the children to list the things they see in it and then arrange the items into classifications based on whatever categories they wish to establish. Initially the teacher should supply the categories. When the children can classify things well, they should be permitted to establish their own categories. The results are compared and contrasted. Very different results may ensue. One child may see modes of transportation and list car, bicycle, and so forth. Another may look at the same picture and classify the items by color. Still another may see words of French or Latin derivation and classify the items that way.

## 2. RECOGNIZING SEQUENCE

MATERIALS: Drawing paper, crayons, paints, camera and film.
PROCEDURE: Give each child an assignment to note something that changes over a day's time, a weekend, or a week. The child must draw or photograph the item to show its changes. The sequence of pictures or photographs is presented to the rest of the group, who must put them together in the correct order. Things that could be used might be an ice cube melting, the sun rising or setting, or the hands of the clock moving.

## 3. RECOGNIZING SEQUENCE

MATERIALS: Drawing paper, crayons, paints.
PROCEDURE: Have the children illustrate the sequential actions in stories.

## 4. ESTABLISHING SEQUENCE

MATERIALS: Drawing paper, crayons, paints.
PROCEDURE: Older children may construct and illustrate a time line of famous artists, architects, sculptors, or fashion designers. The time lines should be compared and contrasted. In this way, the time periods for artists and architects or other types of artistic figures can be compared.

## 5. ESTABLISHING SEQUENCE

MATERIALS: Drawing paper, crayons, paints.
PROCEDURE: Have the children draw the sequential development of an item such as the telephone, the airplane, or the car. An experience that is enjoyed by many children is to project sequential development into the future, determining what an item will be like 50 or 100 years hence and what evolutionary steps will ensue between now and then.

# Drama Experiences and Related Games, Crafts, and Projects

## 1. SEQUENCING MOVEMENT

MATERIALS: Nothing special required.
PROCEDURE: Have the children form a circle. One member starts a movement. The next child does the same movement and adds one more. All the rest do the movements of those preceding and add one more. If a

child cannot remember the sequence, the group can give assistance. Each movement must be repeated exactly. Care should be taken that the group does not pressure a child. Sufficient time should be allowed for each student to try to remember. Children who have a great deal of difficulty should be started close to the beginning (King, 1975, pp. 134, 135).

## 2. Sequencing Movement

MATERIALS: A number of different kinds of simple musical instruments.

PROCEDURE: Use any or all of the following instruments or substitute those that might be appropriate: bongos, maracas, claves, hand clapping, rattle, snare drum, scraper, triangle. List all the instruments and divide the children into groups so that there is one child for each instrument in each group. Provide sheets of paper for each group with the same number of rows as the number of children in the group. Let each group write its own beats for its own orchestra. Each plays its composition (Marsh et al., music center card 4–24b). The groups should be encouraged to add movements to their "orchestra" performance.

An example of a completed composition might look like this:

|            | 1 | 2 | 3 | 4 | 5 | 6 | 7 | 8 |
|------------|---|---|---|---|---|---|---|---|
| Bongo      | x |   |   | x | x | x |   |   |
| Maracas    |   | x | x |   |   |   | x |   |
| Claves     | x |   | x |   | x |   | x |   |
| Cowbell    |   | x |   | x | x |   | x |   |
| Rattle     | x | x | x | x |   |   |   |   |
| Snare drum |   |   |   |   | x | x | x | x |
| Scraper    |   | x | x |   |   |   | x | x |
| Triangle   | x | x | x | x | x | x | x | x |

## 3. Recognizing Sequence

MATERIALS: Nothing special required.

PROCEDURE: Divide the children into groups and give each group an action that requires sequential movements. Actions can include such things as the earth moving around the sun and a plant growing from a seed. Each group plans how to act out the sequence of its event. The remainder of the children must determine what sequence is being portrayed. This activity is well suited for use in science.

## STIMULATING READING

This section includes experiences and activities designed to motivate reading and to further the enjoyment of reading.

## Music Experiences and Related Games, Crafts, and Projects

### 1. NOTING MUSICAL REFERENCES

MATERIALS: Children's stories.
PROCEDURE: Have the children look for allusions to music in literature. The allusions are presented to the group and a discussion is held on how the allusion helped to develop the mood or feeling of the story or assisted in the writing.

### 2. CREATING MUSIC

MATERIALS: A rhythmic poem.
PROCEDURE: Read the poem aloud to the children and then have them read it silently. Discuss how the words flow, when they must be speeded up, when they must be slowed down, and so forth. Ask the children to make up a melody for the poem. The poem "Trees" and its melody can be used as an example. When the melodies are complete, they are shared and the different compositions are compared and contrasted.

### 3. MOTIVATING READING

MATERIALS: Recorded music from a children's story that has been made into a movie, television show, or play.
PROCEDURE: Precede the reading of a particular story with the musical recording of that story. There are many such recordings available, including *Cinderella* and *The Wizard of Oz*.

### 4. CREATING BOOKS

MATERIALS: Blank writing paper, crayons.
PROCEDURE: Have the children create a storybook of a song that tells

a story. That is, a book is made by writing one line of the lyrics of a song on each page and illustrating that line. In some instances, it may be best to write two lines of the lyrics on each page. In addition to the illustrations, the children may include the musical notes on a staff for the lyrics illustrated.

### 5. CREATING STORIES

MATERIALS: Lined poster paper, felt-tip pen.

PROCEDURE: After listening to a concert, watching a ballet, or having any musical experience, create a language experience story with the children.

## Art Experiences and Related Games, Crafts, and Projects

### 1. DRAWING CHARADES

MATERIALS: Drawing paper, crayons, paints.

PROCEDURE: Play a game of "art charades." Two teams are formed. Each team determines some proverbs or well-known phrases from literature. The child who is to present the charade takes a card from the opposite team on which a proverb or a phrase has been written. The child then attempts to draw or sketch it. From the drawing, the child's teammates attempt to guess the proverb or phrase. This activity is well suited to the social studies program since famous phrases from history can be used.

### 2. CREATING ILLUSTRATIONS

MATERIALS: Drawing paper, crayons, paints, glue, cardboard.

PROCEDURE: Have the children create book "pop-ups." Children enjoy this activity and it takes imagination on their parts to determine what should pop up and how. (See figure 3–4.)

### 3. CREATING SCENERY

MATERIALS: Cardboard, tagboard, crayons, paints, and bits and pieces of various items, such as fabric scraps and bits of wallpaper.

PROCEDURE: Have the children construct a miniature stage setting for a story of their choosing. Small groups can be set up with each group producing a setting, or the entire class can divide the tasks and construct one set.

**Figure 3-4**

### 4. ILLUSTRATING STORIES

MATERIALS: Drawing paper, crayons, paints.

PROCEDURE: Have the children create a series of original illustrations for a book. If some books can be obtained from the school or the library which are ready to be discarded, these can be used to good advantage. The children can then make their illustrations and actually place them in the book in place of the original illustrations. To do this, the children must of course read the books.

### 5. ILLUSTRATING STORIES

MATERIALS: Long sheets of paper, rollers, crayons, paints.

PROCEDURE: Have the children make a motion picture of a book or story they particularly enjoyed. They draw a series of pictures, illustrating the story, on a long sheet of paper. The ends of the paper are fastened to rollers. The rollers are turned to bring one picture after another into view.

### 6. RECREATING CHARACTERS

MATERIALS: Manipulative materials, such as clay, soap, and wood plaster.

PROCEDURE: Have the children make sculptures of characters in a book or story whom they particularly liked. The children can each select a different character from a specific story so that every character will be represented.

### 7. RECREATING FASHION

MATERIALS: Fabric, thread, needles, staples.

PROCEDURE: Let the children make their own doll clothes and dress dolls to represent storybook characters. This is a particularly good activity to use when the story setting is from a different time period or country. The activity can be used in social studies too.

### 8. WORKING TOGETHER

MATERIALS: Large poster paper, paints.

PROCEDURE: Have the children make a group mural of a book or story. The emphasis should be on recreating the details and retelling the story. The class or group should be divided into smaller units with each responsible for specific elements. The children should be allowed to determine their smaller units and assign areas of responsibility.

### 9. RECORDING REACTIONS

MATERIALS: Cardboard, drawing paper, crayons, paints.

PROCEDURE: Make a "Book of Books" for the class. Two large cardboard covers are made. As children read books, they record their feelings about the stories read and illustrate their reactions. Their pages are added to the "Book of Books," which is displayed prominently so that other children can look through it when deciding what books they would like to read next for recreation. The emphasis is on the children's reactions to the stories. The story line and characters should not be described.

### 10. ILLUSTRATING MAPS

MATERIALS: Drawing paper, crayons, paints, atlas.

PROCEDURE: Have the children make illustrated maps for a travel story or a story in which the characters move from one place to another. The map representations should be fairly accurate.

### 11. RECREATING SCENERY

MATERIALS: Shoe box, scissors, construction paper, small twigs, spools, or other objects needed to make a scene from a book.

PROCEDURE: A small round hole is cut in one end of a shoe box. A larger opening is cut in the cover of the box. The child builds a scene from a story inside the box on the opposite end to where the small round hole was cut. When the scene is complete, the cover is put on the box. The hole in the cover allows light to come in so that, by looking through the small round hole, one can view the scene (Taylor et al., 1970, task 39).

### 12. RECREATING FACES

MATERIALS: Round tube containers, scissors, glue, yarn, construction paper, buttons.

PROCEDURE: After reading a story, have each child decide upon a character to select as a secret model. Using the details of the story, each child tries to reproduce the expression, hair coloring, eyes, and so forth, of the secret model. The models are displayed on a table and the rest of the group tries to guess who each face is supposed to represent. This activity can also be used to reproduce historical figures. (Suggested by Taylor et al, 1970, task 93.)

## Drama Experiences and Related Games, Crafts, and Projects

### 1. ACTING OUT STORIES

MATERIALS: Nothing special required.

PROCEDURE: Have the children pantomime or stage a shadow show of a book or story they have read. The emphasis is on body movements. The other children try to guess which book or story is being acted out.

### 2. ACTING OUT TITLES

MATERIALS: Nothing special required.

PROCEDURE: Play a game of charades in which the children enact the titles of stories. This is done in teams with points awarded so that one team is the winner. The children can determine the titles they wish to include.

### 3. ACTING OUT STORIES

MATERIALS: 24-inch × 36-inch cardboard, paint, pencils.

PROCEDURE: Have the children make "character boards." Using the large cardboard, the children draw and paint pictures of story characters. On each character board, holes are cut for the face and arms. The children then act out the story (Straatveit and Corl, 1971, p. 35). (See figure 3–5.)

**Figure 3-5**

### 4. ACTING OUT STORIES

MATERIALS: Puppets.
PROCEDURE: Have the children create puppets of characters and put on a puppet show to illustrate a book or story.

## PROCESSING

The areas included in this section are auditory and visual perception and discrimination, listening, and fine and gross motor skills.

# Music Experiences and Related Games, Crafts, and Projects

### 1. BLENDING SOUNDS

MATERIALS: Any musical instrument.

PROCEDURE: Present a sequence of notes, starting with just two or three and building up the number as the children become more proficient. Keep widening the length of the intervals between the notes and have the children repeat the sequence and blend the notes one after the other. If no instrument is available, the notes can be sung. To add some excitement to the game, the notes, when blended, can be an easily recognizable melody.

### 2. DISCRIMINATING VISUALLY

MATERIALS: Sheet music, paper.

PROCEDURE: Work with the children to be able to (a) identify notes on lines and spaces, (b) compare and contrast different notes such as whole, half, quarter, and eighth, (c) copy notes, rest symbols, flats, and sharps, and (d) reproduce notes from memory.

### 3. HEARING RHYMES

MATERIALS: A number of songs.

PROCEDURE: Have the children listen for rhyming words in songs and identify the rhyming sounds. This can be extended by having the children suggest other words that rhyme with a particular word and writing down all the rhymes heard and thought of.

### 4. FOLLOWING ORAL DIRECTIONS

MATERIALS: Nothing special required; a drum is helpful.

PROCEDURE: Establish a number of different beats. Be certain the children can hear the differences among the beats. Then relate each beat to a specific direction to follow. Three equally spaced beats might mean jump up and down; two beats followed by a long interval and then a third beat might mean skip. The children are divided into groups and each group is given a specific activity. The children listen carefully to the beats, and when they hear theirs, they perform their activity. The beats should change suddenly and quickly, without warning, so the children are forced to listen. The children continue to do their activity for as long as their beat lasts.

## 5. LISTENING ATTENTIVELY

MATERIALS: Song lyrics.

PROCEDURE: Have the children listen to the words of a familiar song with a specific purpose in mind, such as listening for the rhyming words or for three-syllable words. A game can be played, for individuals or groups, to see who can hear the greatest number of rhymes, three-syllable words, and so forth.

## 6. FOLLOWING ORAL DIRECTIONS

MATERIALS: A number of different kinds of simple musical instruments.

PROCEDURE: Assign children different instruments: drums, triangles, harmonicas, scrapers. The children then stand with their backs to the leader, who plays one instrument and gives a direction, such as to turn around, hop, sit down, or jump. All the children who have been assigned the instrument that was played must do as they have been told. In this activity, the children are required to identify the instrument purely by listening to it and recognizing its sound.

## 7. DISCRIMINATING SOUNDS

MATERIALS: A number of different musical instruments, recorded instrumental songs.

PROCEDURE: A number of simple activities can be used. They include having the children listen to and identify (a) the sounds of different instruments, (b) different sounds or melodies, (c) identical sounds and melodies, and (d) sounds that are high and low, loud and soft, near and far, or slow and fast.

## 8. DISCRIMINATING VISUALLY*

MATERIALS: Pictures of different notes: whole, half, quarter, and eighth.

PROCEDURE: The children are taught to identify the different notes. When they have learned them, a game can be played. A different movement is established for each note as illustrated in figure 3–6. The picture of a note is held up and the children must do as the directions for that note indicate. When the children can do this well, multi-steps, using multiple notes, can be put on each picture.

*Contributed by Claudette Donnelly, Saunderstown, R.I.

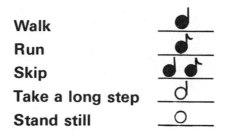

| | |
|---|---|
| **Walk** | |
| **Run** | |
| **Skip** | |
| **Take a long step** | |
| **Stand still** | |

**Figure 3-6**

### 9. REFERENCES

PALMER, HAP. Volume 2, #AR522. The album includes two visual discrimination activities. "Words on the Board" requires the children to match word cards to words on the board as the lyrics of the song direct them. "One Shape, Three Shapes" requires the children to match their shapes to the correct one on the board as the teacher points to shape names in the story. In addition, in volume 1 (#AR514) and volume 2, Palmer includes a number of activities that require listening to the music and following the directions.

JANIAK, WILLIAM. #7016, 7017, 7018, 7019, 7020, 7021, 7022, 7023, and 7024. A number of music activities suitable for developing various processing skills are included.

LEVIN, GAIL, LEVIN, HERBERT, and SAFER, NANCY. Tapes. This is a basic perceptual-motor skill development program. A teacher's guide is included in the program.

VISCO, SUSAN. *Visco Developmental Training Program in Auditory Perception.* This tape program is designed for readiness programs and for remedial reading children who have special needs in auditory perception, language, and learning. The program serves kindergarten through third grade.

REICHARD, CARY L., and BLACKBURN, DENNIS B. 1973, p. 192. A number of songs and activities for developing processing skills are suggested.

## Art Experiences and Related Games, Crafts, and Projects

### 1. FOLLOWING ORAL DIRECTIONS

MATERIALS: Colored construction paper, scissors, large sheets of paper, glue.

PROCEDURE: Each student is directed to cut colored paper into pre-determined shapes and sizes. Each pupil is also given a large sheet of paper and paste. When everyone is ready, one half of the group is blindfolded and the other half watch. The roles are switched when the activity is over, and then the experience is repeated. The teacher or leader gives directions to the blindfolded students telling them where to place each shape on the large paper. When all the shapes have been placed, the blindfolds are removed and the works are examined, discussed, and compared. The importance of listening carefully is emphasized (King, 1975, p. 180).

## 2. DEVELOPING MOTOR ABILITIES

MATERIALS: Fabric, thread, needles, drawing paper, crayons, paints, clay, wire, wood blocks.

PROCEDURE: A number of art activities help to develop fine and gross motor coordination. Some that can be used include (a) quilting, (b) coloring or painting within the lines, (c) making wood or potato cuts of words, and (d) such tracing and manipulating experiences as making clay letters and bending wire into letters and words.

## 3. DEVELOPING MOTOR ABILITIES

MATERIALS: Large sheets of white paper, crayons, paints.

PROCEDURE: The large sheets of paper are pinned up on the wall. Each child stands up against one sheet, and another child traces around the entire figure. When all the children have had turns at being both the model and the tracer, they color or paint their own figures (Kranz and Deley, 1970, p. 87).

# Drama Experiences and Related Games, Crafts, and Projects

## 1. DISCRIMINATING SOUNDS

MATERIALS: Nothing special required.

PROCEDURE: The group is divided in half. One group is blindfolded. The second group arranges itself as obstacles that the first group will have to go under, around, and through. The children should create and use as many levels and shapes as possible. A sighted person sets the blindfolded group in the correct direction and warns them about chairs, and so forth, in the way. Soft music may be played in the background. Each person-obstacle can make a specific sound to indicate if the obstacle is high or low or whether the blindfolded child should go over, around, or under. A specific number of sounds should be established so that the children know when they are finished. The children may hold on to each other or go separately (King, 1975, pp. 141, 142).

## 2. Discriminating Sounds

MATERIALS: Tape recorder.

PROCEDURE: Tape record each child's voice speaking the same saying or phrase. Have the children listen to the recordings and classify each voice as high, low, or middle. Be certain that the students can each hear the differences. After the voices are classified, these classifications can be used to divide the voices for choral speaking. Choral speaking is discussed in chapter 4, "Oral-Language Experiences," in the verbal language section.

## 3. Moving Rhythmically

MATERIALS: Nothing special required.

PROCEDURE: Have the children form a circle, holding hands. Each child counts off "one, two, one, two" until everyone has a number. The teacher calls out the directions. Number ones lean out, number twos lean in, and so forth. Four counts are taken to lean out and four counts to lean in the opposite direction. Four more counts are taken to come to the center again. The teacher starts the group by giving four counts to set the beat. At first the teacher should count loudly. Gradually the teacher works to the point where each child can count silently. The circle of children should stand as close together as possible to make the task easier. Other directions that can be used include bending down and stretching up (King, 1975, p. 258).

## 4. Developing Motor Abilities

MATERIALS: Recorded music, skip rope.

PROCEDURE: A number of basic activities can be used. Among these are (a) walking to tapped rhythm, (b) clapping in unison, (c) walking to music, (d) walking and running to changing tempos, (e) moving to music, (f) skipping rope to music, (g) hopping to music, (h) galloping, tiptoeing, swaying to music, (i) creating a repetitive pattern of movement, such as walk-run-hop, walk-run-hop, (j) clapping a pattern established by someone else, and (k) marching to music, stomping when the music is loud and tiptoeing when it is soft.

## 5. Sharpening the Senses

MATERIALS: Tapes or records, bags or boxes, items with distinctive odors, textures, or sounds.

PROCEDURE: The environment is set up by including things in bags or boxes which have distinctive odors, textures, sounds; eating and drinking items; and so forth. The items are set up on different levels. Half the group is blindfolded. A seeing partner leads each blindfolded child around the room to experience each of the odors, textures, tastes, levels. Soft music is played as the children move about. When the blindfolded child has experienced all the items, the roles are reversed. When everyone has had a turn, a discussion is held about what was smelled, felt, and so forth. In addition, the discussion can be expanded to include what it felt like to be the leader and what it felt like to be the follower, why the children felt that one was better than the other, which senses were stronger, and which senses were very weak (King, 1975, pp. 188, 189).

## VOCABULARY

Almost every activity described in this book has the potential for increasing vocabulary. This section includes experiences specifically oriented toward expanding word meanings, expanding vocabulary, understanding meaning, using vocabulary, and understanding word relationships.

## Music Experiences and Related Games, Crafts, and Projects

### 1. EXPANDING WORD MEANINGS

MATERIALS: Nothing special required.
PROCEDURE: Introduce musical terms that have different meanings in other contexts. Discuss these words and their musical meanings, and let the children determine as many additional meanings as they can for the words. Terms such as "scale," "staff," and "note" can be used. This can be played as a game, with the winner being the student who can determine the most meanings for the given word. A variation would be to have the children think up musical words that have different meanings in other contexts.

### 2. RECOGNIZING MUSICAL VOCABULARY

MATERIALS: Nothing special required.
PROCEDURE: Have the children write original stories using as many musical terms, in nonmusical ways, as possible. When the stories are complete, papers are exchanged and another student attempts to find the hidden musical words.

### 3. Expanding Word Meanings

MATERIALS: Nothing special required.

PROCEDURE: Have the children develop, over a period of time, a list of musical words and their definitions. These can be set up in dictionary form or simply kept on sheets of loose-leaf paper. Additional words and their definitions should be added as they are learned or found.

### 4. Using Vocabulary

MATERIALS: Nothing special required.

PROCEDURE: Have the children identify their favorite stories from a basal reader or from children's literature. Then have the children compose songs using the vocabulary words found in the story and their meanings (Carter and Adams, 1978, pp. 56–58).

### 5. Recognizing Sight Words

MATERIALS: Recorded music, a chair for each child in the group, word cards representing a specific sight word with which the children are having difficulty, flash cards of the words.

PROCEDURE: This game is played like Musical Chairs. Flash cards of the words to be used are taped onto the chairs. Each child is given a flash card with one word on it. The music is turned on and the children march around the chairs. When the music stops, each child sits down on the nearest chair. Then the child checks the flash card against the word on the chair. If the words match, the child remains seated. If not, the game continues with the children who have not yet found a match. The game continues until all the chairs have been taken. The game can be used with homonyms, synonyms, or antonyms as well as words that require a certain amount of visual discrimination, such as "horse" and "house" and "nose" and "noise." This game is a variation of the one described in experience 7 in the word-recognition section earlier in this chapter.

## Art Experiences and Related Games, Crafts, and Projects

### 1. Expanding Word Meaning

MATERIALS: Drawing paper, crayons, paint.

PROCEDURE: Have the children draw pictures to make an illustrated vocabulary book for each subject area. A comparison can be made of the meanings of the words in the different areas, for example, "cell" in biology and "cell" in social studies.

## 2. UNDERSTANDING MEANINGS

MATERIALS: Drawing paper, crayons, paint.

PROCEDURE: Have the children make a list of opposite-word pairs and then find or draw pictures to illustrate the differences. The pictures are shared when completed, and the other children attempt to determine which word pairs each picture represents.

## 3. EXPANDING VOCABULARY

MATERIALS: Nothing special required.

PROCEDURE: Introduce the game of Extension. This game can be used with either art or music and is applicable to every content area. Start by writing a word such as "painter" on the board in the center of a large rectangle. Each child is then asked to list every word that comes to mind related to that key word. After sufficient time, they are asked to read their lists aloud. Their words are written around the outside of the rectangle. No word is refused, but each child must explain the relationship between the word given and the key word. Each word is defined and discussed. Many new words and relationships develop as a result of this activity. (See figure 3–7.)

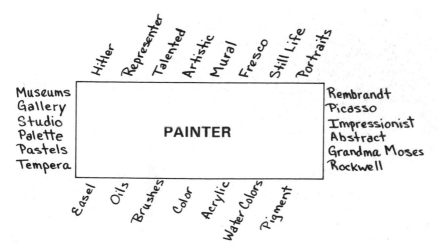

**Figure 3-7**

### 4. EXPANDING VOCABULARY

MATERIALS: Camera, film.

PROCEDURE: The children are asked to take a photograph of something that interests them. They then write fifty words that are shown in or implied by the picture they took. The photographs and vocabulary words are exchanged and shared with others (Waller, 1981, p. 95).

### 5. EXPANDING VOCABULARY

MATERIALS: Reproductions of famous works of art.

PROCEDURE: Tell the children something about the artists and the names of the paintings. After discussing the overall effects of each painting, have the children compare them in respect to style and interpretation. Record the vocabulary words that arise during the discussion and use these as the basis for a vocabulary lesson.

### 6. EXPANDING VOCABULARY

MATERIALS: Items with interesting textures, paper bags, drawing paper, crayons, paint.

PROCEDURE: Have each child select three items with an interesting texture and put them in three different paper bags. The group forms a circle and all the bags are placed in the center. Each student selects a bag and feels the contents without looking. Each child considers what thoughts the textures evoke: attraction, repulsion, memories that come to mind. After each child has had a turn, one of the textures is chosen and discussed more fully with the vocabulary meanings enriched during the discussion. The children then use an art medium to illustrate how they feel about the texture (King, 1975, p. 218).

## Drama Experiences and Related Games, Crafts, and Projects

### 1. EXPANDING WORD MEANINGS

MATERIALS: Nothing special required.

PROCEDURE: Each child is asked to make a movement that represents an action, for example, up and down. The other children think of what the movements represent and then name things that move the same way. For up and down, they might name an elevator, escalator, or thermometer. For things that go around they could mention clock hands, and so forth. This activity can be played as a game, with points given for correct responses.

## 2. EXPANDING WORD MEANINGS

MATERIALS: Nothing special required.
PROCEDURE: The children divide into small groups to make a scenario that will show two or three meanings for a word. Such words as "cell," "host," "bluff," and "stick" could be used. The group acts out its word and the rest of the children determine the word being acted out.

## 3. UNDERSTANDING WORD RELATIONSHIPS

MATERIALS: Nothing special required.
PROCEDURE: The children form a circle. Two children are picked to go into the center. The two children then decide on two antonyms and, using their bodies, demonstrate the antonyms to the rest of the group. The others try to guess the words. Antonyms chosen can be "short" and "tall," "big" and "small," and so forth. Another way to play the game is to have one of the two children act out a word. The second child then figures out the word and acts out its opposite. The two children in the center are not permitted to speak with each other. The game continues until all the children have had a chance to be in the center (Nash et al., 1977, p. 103).

## 4. DEVELOPING CONCEPTS

MATERIALS: Nothing special required.
PROCEDURE: Set up a group of four or five students. Using movements, one person in the group establishes a direction for the rest of the group to follow. The direction can be to move up, down, in, out, over, under, right, or left. Everyone follows the direction but not necessarily using the same movement to accomplish it. When everyone is following the direction, a new person gives a new direction. Sounds and rhythms can complement the movements (King, 1975, p. 155). This activity can also be used to develop concepts.

## 5. EXPANDING WORD MEANINGS

MATERIALS: Nothing special required.
PROCEDURE: Write four words on the board, such as "happy," "sad," "afraid," and "mad." Have the children express them (a) with tone of voice only, using the letters of the alphabet, and responding on a rhythmic beat, (b) in manner of walking, using no speech, (c) with the eyes, face, and arm gestures but with no walking or talking, and (d) with the voice and the entire body, such as stalking or skipping. The leader points to different words as the game moves from one person to another (Nash et al., 1977, p. 34).

6. EXPERIENCING SENSATIONS

MATERIALS: Nothing special required.

PROCEDURE: Let the children explore the feeling of being blown up like a balloon. Have the children move as if they were balloons, were blown up, and then the air was let out. Experiment with the movements created when the air is pumped in and/or let out, slowly and rapidly. Discuss the feelings created and such things as how it might feel to be a balloon floating over a city or over a mountain (King, 1975, p. 110).

# REFERENCES

CARTER, DOUGLAS C., AND ADAMS, JAMES A. "ABC Program." *Music Educators Journal* (January 1978): 56–58.

JANIAK, WILLIAM. *Developing Everyday Skills* and *Songs About Me*. Long Branch, N.J.: Kimbo Educational. Records.

KING, NANCY. *Giving Form to Feeling*. New York: Drama Book Specialists/Publishers, 1975.

KRANZ, STEWART, AND DELEY, JOSEPH. *The Fourth "R": Art for the Urban School*. New York: Van Nostrand Reinhold Co., 1970.

LEVIN, GAIL, LEVIN, HERBERT, AND SAFER, NANCY. *Learning Through Music*. Hingham, Mass.: Teaching Resources Corp. Tapes.

MARSH, MARY VAL; REINHART, CARROLL; SAVAGE, EDITH; BEELKE, RALPH; AND SILVERMAN, RONALD. *The Spectrum of Music with Related Arts*. New York: Macmillan. Teacher's manuals.

NASH, GRACE C.; JONES, GERALDINE W.; POTTER, BARBARA A.; AND SMITH, PATSY F. *The Child's Way of Learning*. Sherman Oaks, Calif.: Alfred Publishing Co., 1977.

PALMER, HAP. *Learning Basic Skills Through Music*. Freeport, N.Y.: Educational Activities. Records.

REICHARD, CARY L., AND BLACKBURN, DENNIS B. *Music Based Instruction for the Exceptional Child*. Denver: Love Publishing Co., 1973.

SOSNOWSKI, FRANK. "Report Making the Cartoon Way." *Grade Teacher* (March 1975): 75–77.

STRAATVEIT, TYYNE, AND CORL, CAROLYN. *Early Art Lessons, K–6*. West Nyack, N.Y.: Parker Publishing Co., 1971.

TAYLOR, FRANK D., ARTUSO, ALFRED A., AND HEWETT, FRANK M. *Creative Art Tasks for Children*. Denver: Love Publishing Co., 1970.

VISCO, SUSAN J. *Visco Developmental Training Program in Auditory Perception*. Freeport, N.Y.: Educational Activities. Tapes.

WALLER, VICTORIA MILLER. "Lights, Camera, Action! The Camera as a Tool for Teaching Reading." In *Motivating Reluctant Readers*, edited by Alfred J. Ciani. Newark, Del.: International Reading Association, 1981, pp. 90–97.

# CHAPTER 4

# Oral-Language Experiences

THE EXPERIENCES IN THIS CHAPTER are divided into two broad categories: nonverbal expression and verbal expression. Creative drama has a great deal to offer in these areas and plays a larger role than music or art.

## NONVERBAL EXPRESSION

This section contains experiences and activities that demonstrate (1) the importance of facial expression and bodily movement to speech, and (2) the fact that speech is not the only way to communicate.

### Music Experiences and Related Games, Crafts, and Projects

1. LEARNING OTHER FORMS OF COMMUNICATION

MATERIALS: Items from which drums can be made, such as oatmeal boxes, margarine tubs, or coffee cans.

PROCEDURE: The children are asked to make and decorate various kinds of drums. The drums should represent those used by different countries or cultures during different time periods. When the drums are completed, the children should do some reading to determine how and for what purpose each drum was used. Each child then reports to the rest of the group by playing the drum to demonstrate the particular signal and explaining the meaning of the drumbeat. This activity can also be used in the social studies program (Longo, 1975, Bicentennial Card). A natural outgrowth of this activity, once the children have learned that drums were used to send messages and to communicate, is to have the students create their own messages and commands for use in the classroom or on the playground.

## 2. LEARNING OTHER FORMS OF COMMUNICATION

MATERIALS: Recorded classical music, filmed dance production.

PROCEDURE: Have the children listen to some classical music with their eyes closed. Then ask such things as, "What is the music telling you?" "What impressions did you receive?" "What feelings were aroused?" Discuss how the music communicated these things. Play another classical piece that will evoke different feelings. Repeat the discussion and then compare and contrast the two compositions. The same procedure can be used with filmed dance productions. The children should become aware that speech is not the only way to communicate.

# Art Experiences and Related Games, Crafts, and Projects

## 1. COMMUNICATING WITHOUT LANGUAGE

MATERIALS: A television set or foreign-language film.

PROCEDURE: Have the children watch a television story with the sound turned all the way down. Or, have them watch a foreign-language film that has no subtitles. When the viewing is over, discuss what was happening, how the children knew what was happening, the events that occurred, and so forth. Lead them to see that the art form in itself is a means of communication and that communication can take place without words.

## 2. LEARNING OTHER FORMS OF COMMUNICATION

MATERIALS: A number of abstract paintings.

PROCEDURE: Have the children examine an abstract painting. Then discuss such things as what the artist was telling viewers, what feelings were evoked, how were ideas communicated by the artist, and so forth. Have the children examine a second abstract painting that arouses different feelings. Repeat the discussion and then compare and contrast the two. The same procedure can be used with paintings representing different styles. If desired, scenic photographs can be used and a discussion held on what the photographer wanted to communicate.

## Drama Experiences and Related Games, Crafts, and Projects

### 1. INTERPRETING WRITTEN LANGUAGE

MATERIALS: Descriptive poems.
PROCEDURE: Read a descriptive poem. A good poem to use is one that contains such obvious movement suggestions as slithering snakes, pounding waves, or roaring winds. Then have the children illustrate the poem through body movement. As the poem is reread, the children move for the particular phrases or lines that indicate a specific movement. When the children can do this well, poems can be used in which the movement suggestions are not as apparent.

### 2. SPEAKING WITHOUT WORDS

MATERIALS: Nothing special required.
PROCEDURE: Have two children conduct a nonverbal conversation using a part of their bodies to talk to someone else's identical part. Elbows can talk to elbows, knees to knees, shoulders to shoulders. Different parts of the body should be given different emotional qualities, such as angry elbows or sad shoulders. When the activity is over, have the children discuss how they felt, what was difficult about the expression, and what was easy (King, 1975, pp. 138, 139).

### 3. INTERPRETING FACIAL EXPRESSION*

MATERIALS: Nothing special required.
PROCEDURE: Present a variety of situations to which the children must react with facial-expression changes. Examples of what can be posed are: "How do you think you would react if . . .

Someone told you the hamburger you just ate was made of dog food?
Someone was talking to you in a foreign language you did not understand?
A horse stepped on your lunch?
You won a trip to Disney World?

Someone poured cold water over your head?
You were getting a tooth pulled?

Through activities of this type, the children learn that oral communication involves not only speaking but bodily and facial expression as well.

*Contributed by Maureen Harrington, Westerly, R.I.

## 4. Speaking Without Words

MATERIALS:  Nothing special required.
PROCEDURE:  The children are paired off. Then, without using language, one student in the pair must convey a feeling about something to the other one. Gibberish may be used. The incident should involve telling something about which the child feels strongly. Following the communication, discuss how much of it depended upon gesture, body movement, inflections, and so forth. Talk about what kinds of things are communicated easily and what kinds of things are difficult to communicate (King, 1975, pp. 126, 127).

## 5. Identifying Situations

MATERIALS:  Nothing special required.
PROCEDURE:  Working in groups of four to six, the children pantomime the kind of imaginary environment they are in. No words are used. The other groups should be able to identify the environment: hot or cold, hilly or flat, and whether there are trees, water, mountains, and so forth. The more details that are elicited, the richer the experience will be. Both indoor and outdoor environments should be used (King, 1975, pp. 191, 192).

## 6. Eliciting Feelings

MATERIALS:  Nothing special required.
PROCEDURE:  Give such directions as, "You are moving on ice" or "You are swimming in mollases." Each child in the group moves individually and tries to follow the directions. The group then gets together to discuss how each one felt when moving in the particular way. A group painting can be made to express the feeling. The finished work would be shared and discussed with other groups. The directions may include movements requiring physical contact as well as movements without physical contact (King, 1975, pp. 190, 191).

### 7. COMMUNICATING WITHOUT LANGUAGE

MATERIALS: Nothing special required.

PROCEDURE: Divide the children into groups of four or five. Present a story plot to each group to act out using no words. The remaining children watch each performance and try to determine the plot being depicted. A discussion is held to determine what might have been done differently, how, and where the performance was successful and unsuccessful.

### 8. COMMUNICATING WITHOUT LANGUAGE

MATERIALS: Nothing special required.

PROCEDURE: Set up children in pairs of two. One student in each pair is selected to be the leader. The two children stand facing one another. The leader then makes a movement of some kind. The second child in the pair must try to anticipate the first child's movements and make the same movements, but in mirror image. If the leader waves the right hand, the follower waves the left hand, and so forth. The follower attempts to do the movements at the same time as the leader. When four or five movements have been attempted, reverse the roles. The pairs are then brought together to discuss how they felt being the leader, how they felt being the mirror image, what was difficult, and what clues they got to anticipate movements.

### 9. COMMUNICATING WITHOUT LANGUAGE

MATERIALS: Nothing special required.

PROCEDURE: One leader is selected and the rest of the group face the leader. The leader makes various movements. The group must make the same movements, but in the opposite direction. If the leader takes two steps forward, the group takes two steps backward. The movements of the group are made after the leader has completed a movement. This is not an easy activity. It may take a bit of practice before the children are able to think in reverse. Following a series of movements, a discussion is held about the difficulties encountered. The role of leader should be rotated among the children.

## VERBAL EXPRESSION

This section includes a number of experiences for communicating with language. They include choral speaking, debating, responding to sounds and words, improvisation, and dramatics. In addition, since puppetry plays such a large role in drama, a full discussion is included on how to make puppets.

## Music Experiences and Related Games, Crafts, and Projects

### 1. SPEAKING WITH MUSICAL ACCOMPANIMENT*

MATERIALS: A variety of instrumental recordings.

PROCEDURE: Have a student select a story to be told. The child reads the story and then prepares a verbal presentation. In addition to preparing a way to tell the story, the child selects music that will correspond to the story: (a) by nationality, (b) as part of the plot, (c) as an integral part of the story, (d) as an interlude between sections, (e) as a motif for characters, or (f) as background. The child tells the story with the musical background.

A number of different pieces of music or parts of music can be selected. The music may play continuously, may stop at points while the narration continues, and so forth.

*Contributed by Roberta M. Humble, Associate Professor of English, Rhode Island Junior College.

### 2. REPRODUCING LANGUAGE

MATERIALS: A piano or other musical instrument that can accompany singing.

PROCEDURE: All kinds of singing activities promote language development. They include solos, duets, trios, barbershop quartets, and choral work. Children also enjoy singing rounds. Through singing, which is an extension of speech, pronunciation and enunciation can be improved.

### 3. USING SENTENCES*

MATERIALS: Nothing special required.

PROCEDURE: Teach the song "Frère Jacques" using the following words for the leader, the child, and the class:

Leader: Where is _____? (child's name)
           Where is _____?
Child:    Here I am.
             Here I am.

Can you see me _____? (dancing, hopping, skipping, sliding, jumping)
Class:    Yes, we see you _____.
_____ away.
_____ away.

The song is repeated, with the child who was called becoming the new
leader. The new leader selects a different activity. The children receive
practice in asking and answering questions using full sentences.

*Contributed by Sylvia M. Marchetti, Raton, New Mexico.

# Art Experiences and Related Games, Crafts, and Projects

## 1. ANALYZING CRITICALLY

MATERIALS:  A painting, drawing, or sculpture that indicates some
action.

PROCEDURE:  Have the students examine the piece of art carefully.
Then pose the following questions to different students: (a) "What happened just before this?" (b) "What might happen right after this?" (c)
"Who might be involved?" The students each present their views and a
discussion follows.

## 2. IMPROVISING DIALOGUE*

MATERIALS:  Tape recorder, drawing paper, crayons, paint.

PROCEDURE:  A group of four to six students is set up. The students
are seated around a tape recorder and one child is made responsible for
operating the machine. A conflict situation is established, such as:

A mother and father have a child who is on the track team. The child's leg has
been injured recently. The doctor says the runner can use the leg to walk around
but that it is not advisable to run races. The most important race of the year is
coming up. The runner wants to race. Should the parents let their child run?

Each student in the group chooses a role, such as the mother, father,
runner, brother, sister, coach, or doctor. Each must draw a picture of the
character selected. The picture should show how the student feels that
character will look and act. When the drawings are completed, when told
to start, the children discuss the situation playing the roles they have
selected. Five to ten minutes is allowed for the discussion. The tape
recorder is used to record the entire discussion. As each child contributes

to the discussion, the picture of the character being played is held up so that the rest of the group can recognize quickly who is speaking.

After the discussion, the term "conflict" is defined and the group is asked what the conflict of the discussion was. Other terms, such as "climax," "character," "setting," "dialogue," and "plot," are defined. The group then attempts to determine what each of these was in the context of the discussion.

Finally, the tape is played back while the students listen. They are asked to note the overlapping conversation, the unfinished sentences, the tone, and so forth—all the elements of conversation.

This activity can be used for vocabulary development by establishing a conflict situation that will include the vocabulary to be taught. It can also be used for creative writing since the students can be asked to write and illustrate their own conflict situations.

*Contributed by Roberta M. Humble, Associate Professor of English, Rhode Island Junior College.

### 3. DEBATING

MATERIALS: Photographs.
PROCEDURE: Set up a photo debate with one group on the pro side and the other on the con. Each group selects and uses photographs to help win its argument (Waller, 1981, p. 95).

### 4. INTERPRETING MEDIA

MATERIALS: Camera, photographs.
PROCEDURE: The group is divided into two parts. One of the two is to look for and/or photograph the positive aspects of a given topic, such as the school or the environment. The other group looks for the negative aspects of the same topic. The two groups of photographs are displayed, then there is a discussion of media interpretation, that is, how much of what we see pictured can we believe? (Waller, 1981, pp. 95, 96.)

## Drama Experiences and Related Games, Crafts, and Projects

### 1. INTERPRETING LANGUAGE

MATERIALS: Nothing special required.
PROCEDURE: A group of four or five students forms a circle with one student in the center. Each member of the group, in turn, calls out a

direction, such as "Clap your hands." The child in the center follows the direction. The next child then modifies the way that specific part of the body is to be moved, such as "Raise your hands over your head." The activity continues until no one in the group can think of a new way to modify the movement of the part of the body. A new person then comes to the center and the activity begins again with a new direction for a different part of the body.

When the activity becomes too easy, more difficult directions are given, such as "You are old and sick." The second child might then add, "You have fever and are hot." The next one might continue with "You have to take a bad-tasting medicine," and so forth (King, 1975, p. 140).

## 2. Speaking in Chorus

MATERIALS: Poems with a good rhythm.

PROCEDURE: The children are divided into groups in one of the following ways: boys and girls; high, middle, and low voices; solo voices mixed with one of the above combinations. The children are given a poem in which the lines have been divided according to the voice combinations desired. As the children speak the lines of the poem chorally, the teacher directs the group, just as a conductor would direct an orchestra. The teacher maintains the beat for the group, indicates soft and loud places, indicates slower and faster speeds, and so forth. It is best to allow the children time to read the poem silently before the choral speaking begins and to allow time for difficult or new words to be clarified.

The following example shows what one teacher did with A. A. Milne's poem "Disobedience." Three groups of voices are used as well as the entire group together.

| All | James James |
|     | Morrison Morrison |
|     | Weatherby George Dupree |
|     | Took great |
|     | Care of his Mother, |
|     | Though he was only three. |
| Low | James James |
|     | Said to his mother, |
|     | "Mother," he said, said he: |
|     | "You must never go down to the end of the town, |
|     | If you don't go down with me." |
| All | James James |
|     | Morrison's Mother |
|     | Drove to the end of town. |

High    James James
           Morrison's Mother
           Said to herself, said she:
           "I can get right down to the end of the town
           And be back in time for tea."

Middle   King John
           Put up a notice,

All       "Lost or stolen or strayed!
           [loudly]
           James James
           Morrison's Mother
           Seems to have been mislaid.
           Last seen
           Wandering vaguely:
           Quite of her own accord,
           She tried to get down to the end of the town—
           Forty shillings reward!"

Low      James James
           Morrison Morrison
           (Commonly known as Jim)
           Told his
           Other relations
           Not to go blaming him.

Middle   James James
           Said to his Mother,
           "But Mother," he said, said he:
           "You must never go down to the end of the town
           Without consulting me."

All       James James
           Morrison's Mother
           Hasn't been heard of since.
           King John said he was sorry,
           So did the Queen and Prince.

High    King John
           (Somebody told me)
           Said to a man he knew:

Low      "If people go down to the end of the town,
           Well, what can anyone do?"

High    J. J.
           [whisper]
           M. M.
           W. G. Du P.
           Took great

c/o his M****
"M****," he said said he:
All       [start softly, getting louder gradually]
          "You-must-never-go-down-to-the-end-of-the-town-
          If-you-don't-go-down-with-Me!"

Choral speaking is always an excellent activity for developing verbal abilities. All aspects of speech are involved and, since the children are working in groups, no self-consciousness develops.

## 3. Responding to Sounds and Words

Materials: Nothing special required.
Procedure: One student starts this activity by making some sounds. The partner of the student responds by moving according to the actions stimulated by the sounds. Then the first person makes a movement and the partner responds in sounds. A discussion is held about the particular movement evoked by the sound (King, 1975, pp. 178, 179). This activity can be extended to words and phrases. One person says a word or phrase and the other moves to the words. Then a movement is made and the partner responds with the words stimulated by the movement.

## 4. Improvising Dialogue*

Materials: Puppet-making materials.
Procedure: Ask a group of students to work cooperatively to establish and perform a puppet dramatization of an original story. As an aid to writing the story, the following outline is presented:

a. Tell who is in the story.
b. Tell where the story takes place.
c. Tell what the problem is.
d. Tell how the problem is solved.

The use of the outline is important because it establishes the main idea of the drama without limiting the characters or the lines of speech.

When the outline is completed, the students make puppets to represent the various characters in the story. Then the show is presented. Since the students are working from an outline, the dialogue will be improvised.

*Contributed by Kathy McGregor, Narragansett, R.I.

## 5. Making Puppets

Materials: Many and varied. The different materials required for each of the different types of puppets are described below.

PROCEDURE: The children are instructed in how to make the particular kind of puppet and then are allowed to work on their own to develop a puppet of the basic type but with creative additions.

Puppet use is not confined to oral-language development and verbal expression. Puppets are valuable in all areas of the curriculum, and puppet activities are included in every curriculum chapter in this book.

## Spoon Puppets

MATERIALS: Wooden or metal spoons, pipe cleaners, construction paper, fabric scraps, crayons, paint, glue, stapler, yarn.

DIRECTIONS: Draw, paint, or glue paper to the spoon to create a face. The clothing is made from the paper or fabric by cutting out the shape and glueing it onto the spoon. Pipe cleaners may be attached for the arms and legs. A hat and any other appropriate decorations may be added. (See figure 4–1.)

**Figure 4-1**

## Paper Plate Puppets

MATERIALS: Paper plates, crayons or paint, construction paper, yarn, fabric, stick or rolled paper for handle, stapler, paste.

DIRECTIONS:

1. Decorate a paper plate to make a face. Attach the handle. (See figure 4–2.)

**Figure 4-2**

2. Fold the plate in half. Make ears, tongue, and so forth, from construction paper and attach. (See figure 4–3.)

**Figure 4-3**

## Paper Bag Puppets

MATERIALS: Assorted sizes of paper bags, some with flat bottoms; newspapers, cardboard, construction paper, paint, glue, scissors, string, dowel rods, thumbtacks.

DIRECTIONS:

1. Two paper bags are used for the neck and head of an animal. Stuff one bag with crumpled newspaper. Attach the other bag to make the neck. Put the stick into the neck of the bag and fasten. Add ears, eyes, and other features. Paint the animal. (See figure 4–4.)

**Figure 4-4**

2. Use paints and paper to make face. The side of the bag becomes the bottom of the mouth and the edge of the bag's bottom becomes the top of the mouth. To use, place four fingers in the bottom of the bag and use the thumb as a lever to make a talking puppet. (See figure 4–5.)

**Figure 4-5**

3. To make a horned animal, stuff two paper bags of the same size (5 inches × 10 inches is a good size) with newspapers and fit one over the other. Tie with string to secure. Cut horns out of the construction paper and use paper, fabric, or paints for the mouth, nose, and eyes. (See figure 4–6.)

**Figure 4-6**

## Sock Puppets

MATERIALS: Socks, felt, egg cartons, pipe cleaners, coffee stirrers, bottle caps, glue, scissors, rubber bands, needle, thread, stuffing.

DIRECTIONS:

1. See figure 4–7.

1. Cut off toe.

2. Cut toe in half.

3. Tie open end with running stitch.

4. Stuff end to make head. Tie with running stitch to make neck.

5. Stitch ends of toe pieces together.

6. Cut holes in body for thumb and middle finger.

7. Attach sewn toe pieces to body for arms.

8. Finish by decorating with fabric, buttons, yarn.

**Figure 4-7**

2. Stuff a small amount of tissue into two small sections of the sock and secure with rubber bands to make ears. Eyes are made from felt or paper. The mouth is made by pushing the toe of the sock into the palm of the hand after the hand has been inserted into the sock. (See figure 4–8.)

**Figure 4-8**

3. Fold the top of an egg carton in half and push it inside a sock. Glue a tongue, made from red paper or felt, to a coffee stirrer and insert through the toe of the sock and the back of the egg carton. This makes it movable. Decorate with pipe cleaners, bottle caps, and so forth. (See figure 4–9.)

**Figure 4-9**

4. Put a sock over your hand and arm, with your thumb in the heel to push it out under the foot of the sock. Push the toe in to make an indentation. Cut a sponge into a bulb shape and attach it to the sock indentation. Decorate with felt and buttons for eyes, hair, ears. (See figure 4–10.)

**Figure 4-10**

## Tube Puppets

MATERIALS: Tubes or cylinders, construction paper, yarn, paper cups, glue, scissors, coffee stirrers.

DIRECTIONS: Use the tube or cylinder as the body or use the cup as the face. Decorate with construction paper and yarn. (See figure 4–11.)

**Figure 4-11**

### Handkerchief Puppets

MATERIALS: Handkerchiefs or napkins, string, fabric, coffee stirrers, scissors, glue.

DIRECTIONS:

1. Roll one handkerchief or napkin into a ball and place it in the center of the other napkin. Dip coffee stirrer into glue and imbed it into the rolled napkin. Gather the second napkin around the first and tie it with a string around the stirrer. Decorate the face. (See figure 4–12.)

**Figure 4-12**

2. Tie a knot in one corner of the handkerchief to make the head. Tie a scrap of fabric around the neck and the top of the head for scarves. Decorate the face. (See figure 4-12A.)

**Figure 4-12A**

## Finger Puppets

MATERIALS:  Construction paper, yarn, fabric, gloves, glue, scissors.
DIRECTIONS:
1.  Make a small paper cylinder to fit over one finger and decorate. (See figure 4–13.)

**Figure 4-13**

2.  Cut a piece of paper with a hole at the bottom so the fingers can fit through for legs. Decorate. (See figure 4–14.)

**Figure 4-14**

3. Cut out ears, noses, and eyes and glue a set to each finger on a glove to make five little animals, such as mice. (See figure 4–15.)

**Figure 4-15**

4. Turn an old woolen glove inside out. Push up the first and little fingers for the ears. Stuff the head. Decorate the face with fabric, yarn, and buttons. Glue on whiskers. Put a rubber band around the neck. (See figure 4–16.)

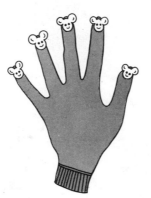

**Figure 4-16**

## String Puppets

MATERIALS: Construction paper, yarn, cardboard, dowels, glue, stapler, scissors, paint.

DIRECTIONS:

1. Cut two construction paper strips 2 × 12 inches. Use two different colors. Glue one strip of one color to a second strip of another color to make an "L." Fold these back and forth across one another to make a spring. Cut eight strips 1 × 12 inches, four of one color and four of another. Make four more springs. Using the largest spring for the body, staple the smaller ones for the arms and legs. Cut a face from construction paper, attach to the body, and decorate. (See figure 4–17.)

**Figure 4-17**

2. Wrap one-quarter of a skein of yarn around a piece of cardboard 10 inches long. Remove the yarn from the cardboard and tie it 1 inch from the top of the skein. Stuff the center to form a head, tying underneath to hold in place. Braid the yarn on the sides for arms. For females, the rest of the yarn is left hanging. For males, the yarn is braided to form two legs on the bottom half of the body. Decorate the face. Use a dowel for handling. (See figure 4–18.)

**Figure 4-18**

## Movable Sock Puppets

MATERIALS: One large sock and four, five, or six smaller ones (depending upon the animal being made), three paint stirrers or flat sticks, fishline or string, stuffing, construction paper, clay, glue, fabric, scissors, needle, thread.

DIRECTIONS:

1. Stuff the large sock and tie with string at a point where the neck will be.
2. Stuff a smaller sock for a tail and attach to the end of the body sock.
3. Stuff four socks for legs. Weight each at the bottom with clay, a rock, or something similar, and attach to the body.
4. Stuff the last sock for a trunk if making an elephant. Attach to face. Paste on facial features and any body features.
5. Attach crossbars to each other firmly. Attach string to crossbars and secure to body. (See figure 4–19.)

**Figure 4-19**

## Movable String Puppets

MATERIALS:  #1 darning needle, twenty-four 1-inch styrofoam balls, three 3-inch styrofoam balls, two sticks ¼ × ¾ inch. One of the sticks should be 16½ inches long, the other 14 inches long. Fishline, screw and nut, felt, buttons, sequins, and so forth, to decorate body, glue. (Adapted from the Reilly Romer directions kit.)

DIRECTIONS:

1. Decorate one of the large balls to make a face. Add a beak for birds. (See figure 4–20.)

**Figure 4-20**

2. Thread a needle with a 9-foot length of fishing line. Take a large ball. Insert the needle in the lower third of the ball and through to the other side. Leave even lengths of line on each side. (See figure 4–21.)

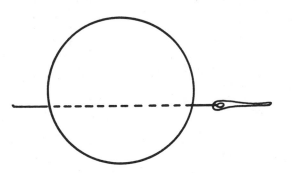

**Figure 4-21**

3. String eight small balls on each side of the line going through the large ball. They make the legs. Take the last large ball and cut it in half. Paste felt on the bottom of each half. Attach a half to the end of each leg, coming through the center and then coming through again about ¼ inch away. Pull both leg lines so that they are even with one another. (See figure 4–22.)

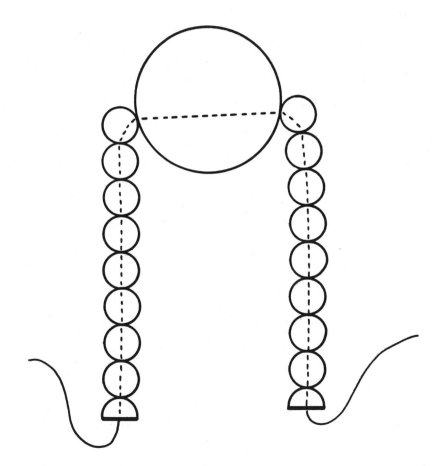

**Figure 4-22**

4. Thread a needle with a 6½-foot line. Thread through the center of the large ball in the opposite direction to the legs and leave equal lengths of line on each side. Thread eight small balls on one end of the line for the neck and end with a large ball for the head by inserting the needle at the back and coming out on the top. (See figure 4–23.)

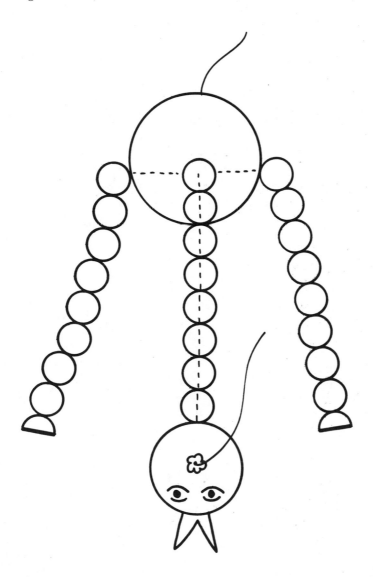

**Figure 4-23**

5.  Insert a sequin on the tail line, curved side down, and glue down. Repeat on the head line. (See figure 4–24.)

**Figure 4-24**

6.  Form a cross with the sticks. Screw together at the center. Tie the puppet to the frame by attaching the tail line to the longest stick at one end and the head line to the other end of the longest stick. Feet lines are attached to short stick. Length of the lines is adjusted to the height of the person using it. Decorate the puppet. (See figure 4–25.)

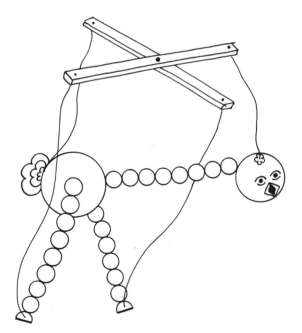

**Figure 4-25**

## Round Ball Puppets

MATERIALS: Potato, round fruit, tennis ball (or similar object), tooth-picks, buttons, fabric, construction paper, glue, yarn, paint.

DIRECTIONS: Decorate a face on the object chosen. Insert or attach a dowel or holder. Add cloth for the body. Place a finger in the hole at the bottom of fruit or hold a dowel. (See figure 4–26.)

**Figure 4-26**

## Balloon Puppets

MATERIALS: Round balloons, pieces of oak tag, paper toweling, liquid paste, paint, masking tape.

DIRECTIONS: Blow up a balloon. Paste oak tag features on with masking tape. Out of oak tag, make a small cylinder for the neck and pull the neck of the balloon through the tube and attach to the outside of the tube. Tear toweling into small pieces and paste a double or triple layer of paper over the entire balloon and features. Allow to dry for a few days. Paint and spray with shellac or plastic coating. Add yarn for the hair. Break the balloon and remove through the neck opening. (See figure 4–27.)

**Figure 4-27**

## 6. REFERENCES

There are a number of books available on puppet making and the use of puppets. The ideas for many of the puppets in this section were suggested by the following references.

KAMPMANN, LOTHAR. *Creating with Puppets.* New York: Van Nostrand Reinhold, 1969.

RESCH, CHERYLL. "Puppet-Making Workshop." St. Thomas, Virgin Islands, 1980.

ROMER, REILLY. *Puppet Kit.* P.O. Box 4398, South Lake Tahoe, Calif. 95705.

ROTH, CARLENE DAVIS. *The Art of Making Puppets and Marionettes.* Radmore, Pa.: Chilton Book Co., 1975.

STRAATVEIT, TYYNE, AND CORL, CAROLYN. *Early Art Lessons, K–6.* West Nyack, N.Y.: Parker Publishing Co., 1971.

# REFERENCES

KING, NANCY. *Giving Form to Feeling.* New York: Drama Book Specialists/Publishers, 1975.

LONGO, VICKY. *Bicentennial Art Cards.* Washington D.C.: The Center for Applied Research in Education, 1975.

WALLER, VICTORIA MILLER. "Lights, Camera, Action! The Camera as a Tool for Teaching Reading." In *Motivating Reluctant Readers,* edited by Alfred J. Ciani. Newark, Del.: International Reading Association, 1981, pp. 90–97.

# CHAPTER 5

# Science Experiences

THE ACTIVITIES IN THIS CHAPTER are presented in two broad categories, biological science and physical science.

## BIOLOGICAL SCIENCE

Within the area of biological science, the following topics are covered: anatomy, botany, zoology (including ornithology, ichthyology, and entomology), and the general areas of environment, health, and nutrition.

### Music Experiences and Related Games, Crafts, and Projects

1. LEARNING ABOUT PLANTS

MATERIALS: Nothing special required.
PROCEDURE: Have the children select specific types of plants and do research on them. The children then write original song lyrics about the plants using well-known melodies. The songs are sung for the rest of the group and a discussion is held. The aim is to describe the plant and its life

cycle, as well as anything unusual or different about it, in the lyrics. The different types of plants should be compared and contrasted.

## 2. LEARNING ABOUT PLANTS

MATERIALS: Costuming materials, simple musical instruments.

PROCEDURE: A class project is set up to present a play, with costumes, original songs, and creative dancing. The theme can be plants or any other topic of interest. Part of such a project is in figure 5-1. The activity was conducted by a third-grade class. In this presentation, one child was the master of ceremonies; however, Clark (1961, p. 60) suggests that this function could be performed by a speaking choir of children different from those who do the singing.

M.C.—This is the story of a little seed that was planted deep in the ground. CHORUS *(sings)*

*(Continued)*

**Figure 5-1.** "The Seed That Grew." *(Reprinted from Instructor, March 1961. Copyright © 1961 by F. A. Owens Company. Used by permission of The Instructor Publications, Inc.)*

M.C.—Soon the cold freezing winds stopped blowing and the white snow melted. High in the blue, blue sky shone the big bright sun. Spring touched the earth with her magic sunbeams and everywhere things began to grow.

SUNBEAMS (*touching the earth with yellow scarfs as they sing*)—

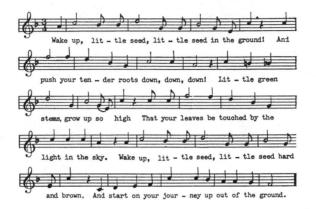

Wake up, lit - tle seed, lit - tle seed in the ground! And push your ten - der roots down, down, down! Lit - tle green stems, grow up so high That your leaves be touched by the light in the sky. Wake up, lit - tle seed, lit - tle seed hard and brown. And start on your jour - ney up out of the ground.

M.C.—One sunny day some children were playing in a wood. They spied the baby plant struggling to push its tender stem trough the soil. All of the children gathered around and cried:

### 3. LEARNING ABOUT ANIMALS

MATERIALS: Nothing special required

PROCEDURE: Have the children compose original songs about animals and their lives and write new words to familiar melodies. The children should be required to do some reference work before writing the songs so that the lyrics contain new information and are factual. The children can also research songs about animals which are already available. The song shown in figure 5–2 is typical of the kinds of songs available and the types of songs the children should strive to write.

### 4. TRACING CHANGE AND GROWTH*

MATERIALS: A number of ballads with standard stanzas.

PROCEDURE: Play and sing a number of ballads. The lyrics may be prerecorded. use standard-stanza ballads, that is, ballads with four-line stanzas in which the lines consist of eight, six, eight, and six syllables each. The children are asked to listen for the consistent rhythm and rhyme in

**Figure 5-2.** "The Little Green Caterpillar." *(Words and music by Malcolm C. Pappin. Reprinted from Instructor, June 1956. Copyright © 1956 by F. A. Owens Company. Used by permission of The Instructor Publications, Inc.)*

all the ballads. When they have determined these, the ballad stanza is written on the board.

Since ballads tell stories, they can be used to tell stories of growth and/or change, such as:

caterpillar to butterfly
sperm/egg to foal
egg to robin
caveman to modern man
waterfall to electricity

This project is applicable to all aspects of science. The students are given a category and asked to write a ballad of their own. The children determine the growth or change story to be told.

As an extension, the students can research, through their parents, when they first began to hold up their heads, reach for things, walk, and talk and write ballads of their own development up to the present. Many skills are involved in this activity: rhythm, accenting, rhyme, syllabication, and vocabulary.

*Contributed by Roberta M. Humble, Associate Professor of English, Rhode Island Junior College.

## 5. Reinforcing Health Skills*

Materials: Nothing special required.

Procedure: Teach the song "Here We Go 'Round the Mulberry Bush." Then have the children write their own stanzas related to some form of health care. The song is an excellent one to use to teach habits of cleanliness and health because it speaks of the way we do something and is an easy song to which children can add stanzas.

When the writing is completed, have the children form a circle and sing. Each child, in turn, sings one original stanza and acts out the motions. The other children then repeat the stanza, and the game moves on to the next child. An attempt should be made to see to it that different topics are covered. The game loses its spark if each stanza describes brushing teeth.

*Contributed by Claudette Donnelly, Saunderstown, R.I.

## 6. References

Janiak, William. *Developing Everyday Skills* and *Songs About Me* (#7016, 7017, 7018, 7019, 7020, 7022, and 7024). A number of songs that help to teach body parts are included. In addition, songs about health can be found in his albums #7017, 7019, 7020, and 7021.

MANN, BARBARA FAY. 1973. This set contains a cassette tape recording of the songs in the book and a printed songbook. The songs include "What You Need to Grow Each Day," "The Food Group Song," "Vitamin Song," "Iron Song," and "The Breakfast Song." Songs such as these can stimulate the writing of original songs by children as well as help to teach the basic science information.

REYNOLDS, MALVINA. 1964. Songs of seasons, rain, animals, growing things, and so forth, are included. It is a good reference for classroom teachers.

DAVIS, BETTE. 1971. Describing insects and musical sounds, this is another reference children may enjoy.

## Art Experiences and Related Games, Crafts, and Projects

### 1. LEARNING ABOUT THE BODY

MATERIALS: Construction paper, scissors.

PROCEDURE: Have the children compare the parts of the body to different basic shapes. Then have them cut the shapes from construction paper and build a person. See if they can take the same shapes and build a person who moves. The children are to note how the shapes must be connected to make them move.

### 2. LEARNING ABOUT THE BODY

MATERIALS: Drawing paper, tape measures.

PROCEDURE: Have the students draw an entire figure or a specific part of the body in proportion to the size of a human being. The students can experiment on themselves to determine the size of the head in relation to the rest of the body, the length of the arms and legs, and so forth. This project can also be used in mathematics in the area of measurement and proportion.

### 3. LEARNING ABOUT THE BODY

MATERIALS: Clay, papier-mâché, construction paper, glue, scissors.

PROCEDURE: Have the children make models of various parts of the body, after studying them. The models should represent an internal view of the part of the body.

### 4. LEARNING ABOUT PLANTS

MATERIALS: A small plot of ground with some foliage.

PROCEDURE: Each child is directed to select a small piece of ground with some foliage on it. It need not be a large piece; even 2 feet × 2 feet or the area between the sidewalk and the curb is sufficient. Then, at least twice a week, over a period of a few months, the child observes the land and the foliage carefully. The observations are made at different times of day. After each observation, the child records the hour of day, the date, the temperature, and exactly what was seen. The child must also illustrate each observation or photograph it. When the observations are completed, the child puts them together to make a nature log and writes a summary of the changes that took place, interesting things observed, and so forth.

This activity tends to make children more aware of nature. They can note the presence or absence of insects, dew, buds, and flowers. They should feel the earth to see if it is soft or hard, if it changes at different times of day or different months, how it feels after a rain. A great deal of learning comes from this project, and there are many ways to expand upon it. One obvious merit of the activity is that it develops a sense of responsibility and conscientiousness. The child cannot forget to observe for an entire week. Once the week is gone, there is no way to go back to see what happened.

### 5. LEARNING ABOUT CHANGE

MATERIALS: Nothing special required.

PROCEDURE: Give the children the following assignment: Determine a living thing that changes and then use any medium they wish to represent the change without using the thing itself. The completed projects are displayed and discussed. The other children attempt to determine what change is being represented and what living thing manifests that change.

### 6. MAKING LEAF PRINTS*

MATERIALS: Newspaper, large pieces of paper, tempera paint, colored ink, small dish, 6-inch popsicle stick, toothbrush, construction paper, paint brushes, crayons, scissors, leaves.

PROCEDURE: There are a number of different ways to make leaf prints. In most cases a leaf press is needed. The press is handy for drying out and flattening leaves before printing. To make a leaf press, 50 or 60 sheets of newspaper cut into 12-inch × 18-inch sizes are stacked into a pile. They can be bound together at one side between two narrow strips of wood and nailed through. Or, the sheets can be laced together with a piece of string. In order to lace the sheets, they will first have to be punched. After the string is laced in and out of the punched holes, the ends are knotted securely.

*Contributed by Claudette Donnelly, Saunderstown, R.I.

## Leaf Spatters*

Spread a large piece of paper over the table or working area to protect it. Pour thinned tempera paint of colored ink into a small dish. Dip an old toothbrush into the paint or ink. Use a 6-inch stick to scrape the toothbrush. The children must be instructed to scrape the stick through the brush toward them, not away from them. This makes the bristles of the brush snap back away from them to spatter the paint or ink outward, not inward. It is best to have the children practice first, using water. The leaf is placed on construction paper and the ink or paint is spattered on and around the leaf. The finer the spatter, the more effective the print.

*Contributed by Claudette Donnelly, Saunderstown, R.I.

## Whole-Leaf Prints*

Cover the table with paper. Then, using jars of tempera paint and brushes, demonstrate how to brush paint on the back side of pressed leaves. When the leaves are painted, place them, paint side down, on a 9-inch × 12-inch piece of paper. With a second piece of paper placed down over the leaf, press down with one hand carefully. Then lift the paper and the leaf. The shape of the leaf and the veins will remain. A single leaf or a leaf design pattern can be made.

*Contributed by Claudette Donnelly, Saunderstown, R.I.

## Multiple-Leaf Prints

Place a few leaves, ferns, or twigs on newspaper. Brush tempera over them. Place the painted things on another piece of newspaper, painted side up, and press construction paper on top. Lift the construction paper and allow to dry. Vary the activity by trying different colors of construction paper (Taylor et al, 1970, task 21).

## Whole-Leaf Prints

Place flat newspapers on the table or desk for padding. Put a leaf on the padding and cover with a sheet of newsprint. Rub the side of a crayon across the top of the newsprint. Mount the leaf print on construction paper. Vary this by using a number of leaves at one time (Taylor et al, 1970, task 64).

## 7. USING LEAF PRINTS*

MATERIALS: Construction paper, glue, pressed leaves, leaf prints.

PROCEDURE: Have the children make leaf-lets out of the pressed leaves or leaf prints. Construction paper, cut into any size, is folded either vertically or horizontally to make a card. The pressed leaves are layed out first for placement and then glued to the construction paper with a crafts glue. A piece of paper is placed over the glued leaf and pressed down on it to secure the leaf. With leaf prints, paste them onto the construction paper. When the card is completely dry, a message is added. (See figures 5–3 through 5–6.)

*Contributed by Claudette Donnelly, Saunderstown, R.I.

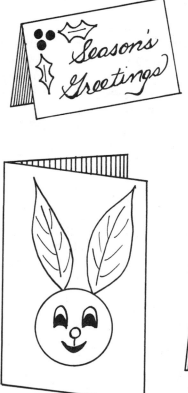

**Figures 5-3 through 5-6**

## 8. LEARNING ABOUT LEAVES*

MATERIALS: Leaves, hairbrush or shoe brush, pounding board.

PROCEDURE: Make a pounding board by tacking a piece of old carpet, about 8 inches × 10 inches, on top of a plank. The leaf is put on the board, top side up, and held firmly with one hand. Using the brush, the child taps firmly until all the fleshiness is worn away. Every once in a while, the leaf should be turned over and its underside tapped. After about ten minutes, the leaf should be held up to the light to see what progress is being made. When the children do this stripping of green leaves down to their skeletons, they discover the delicate veins that plants use to carry the raw materials they make into food.

Leaf skeletons can be preserved by mounting them in a scrapbook, gluing them to a windowpane, or placing them between two pieces of glass or between sheets of clear paper.

*Contributed by Claudette Donnelly, Saunderstown, R.I.

## 9. LEARNING ABOUT LEAVES*

MATERIALS: A bulletin board, large piece of brown paper, dried colored and brown leaves.

PROCEDURE: Sketch and cut out a large treetrunk and branches from the brown paper. The tree size should be about one-third the size of the bulletin board. The children are asked to bring in dried colored and brown leaves. These can be stapled to the tree on the bulletin board. Before the leaves are tacked on, discuss their sizes and shapes and let the children identify the different kinds of leaves. Older children can expand this activity to learn tree identification from the leaf shapes and to collect pieces of wood from the different kinds of trees. They can also explore how the different kinds of wood are used. (See figure 5–7).

*Contributed by Claudette Donnelly, Saunderstown, R.I.

## 10. RECOGNIZING PARTS

MATERIALS: Drawing paper, crayons, paints, scissors.

PROCEDURE: Have the children draw an animal, bird, insect, or plant and then divide the picture into jigsaw puzzle parts. Each part should be labeled with a feature of the item. The picture is then cut apart and exchanged so that another child can put it together (Kaplan et al, 1973, p. 121).

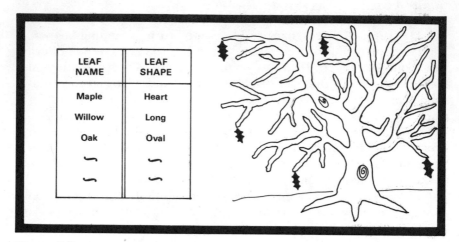

| LEAF NAME | LEAF SHAPE |
|-----------|------------|
| Maple | Heart |
| Willow | Long |
| Oak | Oval |

**Figure 5-7**

## 11. RELATING LIFE TO THE ENVIRONMENT

MATERIALS: Drawing paper, construction paper, crayons, paints.

PROCEDURE: Have each child create a mask for a monster or an animal. When the artwork is completed, the children must determine where their monster or animal lives, what it looks like, what it eats, and so forth. Simple art props can be used to actually create the item. Problems are posed, such as how this animal would differ if it lived at the bottom of the ocean, on the top of a mountain, in the desert, and so forth (King, 1975, p. 121).

## 12. UNDERSTANDING LIFE CYCLES*

MATERIALS: White drawing paper, paste, crayons, paints, scissors, string, coat hanger.

PROCEDURE: After a series of lessons on the life cycle of moths and butterflies, each child takes a sheet of white drawing paper and divides it into four sections. The children then draw within or paste pictures onto each section to represent the four stages in the life cycle: egg, caterpillar, chrysalis or cocoon, butterfly or moth. The children should be allowed to choose the kind of moth or butterfly, such as the Monarch butterfly or the Isabella moth. The colors used to portray the butterfly must be accurate. This activity is best carried on during the fall since cocoons and chrysalises are found easily then.

The completed pictures of the four stages are cut out and attached to strings that are then attached to a coat hanger to make a mobile. The strings should be of different lengths. (See figure 5–8.)

*Contributed by Carolyn Gardiner, North Kingstown, R.I.

**Figure 5-8**

## 13. CAMOUFLAGING*

MATERIALS: Color swatches, drawing paper, crayons, paints.

PROCEDURE: Give each child a swatch of color. Then take the children outside; a park is perfect. Instruct each child to place the swatch somewhere in the area, but not hidden, where the color of the area is similar to the color of the swatch so that it is difficult to see the swatch. After all the swatches have been placed, the children meet in a central location. They are then given three minutes to find as many color swatches as possible, excluding their own. When the activity is completed, discuss which colors were the easiest to find, which were the most difficult, and why. Relate the game to how certain animals use their colors to camouflage themselves. Explain that certain animals undergo color changes, according to their environment, so that they are more difficult to see.

As a concluding activity, the children can make booklets of animals that may be camouflaged. They may draw or cut out the pictures. The animals should be portrayed in their natural habitats. The children should research these animals themselves.

*Contributed by Barbara Stock, North Kingstown, R.I.

## 14. Learning About Birds

MATERIALS: Two pie tins, large nail, hammer, clothesline, 1-pound coffee can with lid, birdseed.

PROCEDURE: Punch a small hole in the center of both of the pie tins and in the lid and bottom of the coffee can. Knot the end of the clothesline and, starting from the bottom of one pie pan, thread upward through the pie pan, through the bottom of the coffee can, through the lid of the coffee can, and through the second pie pan. Tie at the top. Put bird seed in the lower pie pan and hang the feeder in a tree (Taylor et al., 1970, task 113). The children should note types of birds that come to feed, their activities, and so forth.

## 15. Understanding the Environment

MATERIALS: Poster paper, crayons, paints.

PROCEDURE: Have the children create a set of posters promoting good environmental changes and discouraging bad changes. In order to do this, they must first discuss the environment, what is meant by a bad change, and why it is bad.

## 16. Understanding the Environment

MATERIALS: Nothing special required.

PROCEDURE: Have the children collect materials found in the environment and create an art form from them. Each piece of art should show one of the following:

    a. How ugly the environment is
    b. How beautiful the environment is
    c. How the environment makes them feel
    d. How joyous the environment is
    e. How sad the environment is
    f. How time changes the environment

## 17. USING THE ENVIRONMENT

MATERIALS: Nothing special required.

PROCEDURE: Instruct the children to go outside and find something that can be used as a tool to create some work of art. They must bring it to class and use it to create an art piece. Following this activity, the children discuss the art pieces created in reference to what tools were used and what the art pieces show.

## 18. RELATING ART TO REALITY

MATERIALS: A variety of paintings.

PROCEDURE: Have the children examine art works looking for the accuracy of the portrayals of specific flowers, trees, insects, and animals. Note the portrayal of these things in modern and abstract works. Discuss and compare these. As an extension, have the children find and bring in paintings to examine.

## 19. BUILDING SCIENCE VOCABULARY

MATERIALS: Drawing paper, crayons, paints.

PROCEDURE: Have the students make illustrated dictionaries of science terms. Sufficient space should be left so that new words and meanings can be added. A number of dictionaries can be made so that the children have one for each of the specific areas being studied. As an extension to this project, the students can note those words that have different meanings in other content areas.

## 20. LEARNING ABOUT THE BODY*

MATERIALS: White butcher paper, pencils, crayons

PROCEDURE: Give each child a body-sized sheet of white butcher paper. Have the children take turns outlining each others' bodies with a crayon. Then, based on what specifically is being studied, have the children fill the outlines in with such things as various parts of the body, parts of the digestive system, or parts of the circulatory system. Reference materials and models should be available so that the children can get a better idea of the size and placement of each item. The finished drawings should be compared and contrasted.

*Contributed by Susanne Shindler, Incline Village, Nevada, and Christy Ocskay, Reno, Nevada.

## Drama Experiences and Related Games, Crafts, and Projects

### 1. UNDERSTANDING THE PULSE*

MATERIALS: Stopwatch, recorded music of different tempos.

PROCEDURE: Teach the children how to take their pulses or how to take another child's pulse. The following steps are then followed:

a. All the children rest for five to ten minutes. Their pulse rates are taken and are recorded as the resting rates.
b. The children form a circle and walk in four-quarter time to a recording such as "I've Been Working on the Railroad." They walk in time for two minutes. As soon as they stop, their pulse rates are taken again and recorded.
c. The children then march in a circle to a march tempo of six-eighths or two-quarter time, such as "When the Saints Come Marching In." After marching for two minutes, they stop and immediately take and record their pulse rates.
d. The children then jog in a circle to two-quarter time music, such as "Buffalo Gal." After jogging for two minutes, they stop and immediately take and record their pulse rates.

The children must all stop and start at the same time. A stopwatch must be used. As the different pulse rates are recorded, the children should begin to observe that as their activity increases, so, too, do their pulse rates. A discussion should follow on what is happening in the blood vessels due to the increase in activity.

The results obtained from the taking of the pulse rates can be recorded in the form of a chart or graph. In addition, the children can write up the experiment in scientific form.

Musical terms can be added to the experiment. The tempo of walking is "lento," of marching is "moderato," of jogging is "allegretto." The gradual decrease in the pulse rate is "ritard" and the gradual increase is "accelerando."

The children might also be asked to take their pulse rates again after a sufficient rest period. Another extension of this activity is to experiment with different kinds of actions to see if the pulse rate is affected; for example, singing while moving may bring about a different result from just moving while silent. The children can also be asked to find songs with different types of movement, particularly songs that gradually get faster or gradually get slower.

*Contributed by Barbara Stock, North Kingstown, R.I.

## 2. Learning About Plants

MATERIALS: Nothing special required.

PROCEDURE: Have the children determine movements that make them look like a particular plant or represent the growth of a plant. Some plants have buds that open, some start from seeds, others begin from bulbs, and so forth.

## 3. Reacting to Sensory Perceptions*

MATERIALS: Lemonade, food coloring.

PROCEDURE: Prepare a number of different glasses of lemonade, each with a different food coloring added. One group may get a glass of black liquid, another red, another green. Do this without letting the children see what is happening. Then divide the children into groups and have each member of the group pour some of the liquid into a small paper

Listening to science songs can be an enjoyable activity as well as a learning experience for children. (Reprinted by permission of the Montessori School, Iowa City, Iowa. Photograph by Rex Honey.)

cup and taste it. All individuals in each group must record their reactions. After everyone is finished, bring the groups together to discuss their reactions to what they tasted. Then tell them that they all drank the same thing, and have each of the students taste the lemonade in its original form. Discuss how sight affects taste. Relate this experience to other food items liked and disliked by the children. An extension of this activity would be to have each group taste each of the different-colored liquids and record its reaction. Each group could then determine which was the best tasting, which the worst, and so forth, before coming together for a discussion with the other groups and before being told that each of the liquids was lemonade.

*Contributed by Roberta M. Humble, Associate Professor of English, Rhode Island Junior College.

# PHYSICAL SCIENCE

The experiences described in this section include astronomy, geology, physics, and such general topics as seasons, the spectrum, inventions, and nature.

## Music Experiences and Related Games, Crafts, and Projects

### 1. NOTING SCIENTIFIC ACCURACY

MATERIALS: Nothing special required.
PROCEDURE: Have the children find songs about heavenly bodies or songs that include references to heavenly bodies. Then have them analyze them for accuracy. In the song "Deep in the Heart of Texas," for example, the lyrics state, "The stars at night/are big and bright. . . ." The children should discuss: Are the stars different in Texas? Are they bigger, brighter? The children can then compile a list of inaccuracies in musical lyrics and discuss why they may occur.

### 2. LEARNING ASTRONOMY

MATERIALS: Drawing paper.
PROCEDURE: Play a game in which each child must find as many song titles as possible that contain the name of a heavenly body. The children then make astronomical scrapbooks with the names of the songs next to

the picture and description of each heavenly body. Points can be awarded to children who find the most titles or the greatest variety of heavenly bodies.

### 3. Learning About Sound

MATERIALS: A triangle and a drum.

PROCEDURE: Have primary-grade children experiment with a triangle and a drum to determine what part of the instrument is making the sound when the instrument is tapped. The children should feel the vibrations. Let them experiment with tapping the triangle with different kinds of things, such as a spoon, a wooden stick, and a nail and note the differences in the sounds obtained. The children should discuss these differences and hypothesize about why they occur.

### 4. Understanding Sounds*

MATERIALS: Xylophone, shoe box, rubber bands, eight test tubes, water, test tube stand, piano.

PROCEDURE: Strike various bars on the xylophone. Discuss the differences in the sounds heard. Lead the children to see that low sounds are produced when the long bars are struck and high sounds when the short bars are struck. In addition, the longer the bar, the lower the sound and, conversely, the shorter the bar, the higher the sound.

Take a shoe box and put rubber bands across the opening, being certain that some of the bands are tighter and wider than others. Strum the bands and have the children note the different sounds produced by the wider and thinner, looser and tighter bands.

Fill eight test tubes with water, each filled with a different amount. Let the children blow across the top of the tubes, which are held firmly in a stand. Compare the different sounds based on the different amounts of water.

Discuss what causes sound. When the children understand, introduce the musical scale. Play the xylophone again, letting the children hear the scale. Then play the scale again on the piano or some other instrument. The children should learn that each note in the scale is a little higher than the one below.

As a result of this activity, the children should learn what causes high and low sounds, how notes are made up of sounds, and how the scale is made up of notes.

A good song for teaching the scale is:

c = I know a little pussy
d = Her coat is silver gray
e = She lives down in the meadow
f = Not very far away
g = She'll always be a pussy
a = She'll never be a cat
b = For she's a pussy willow
c = Now what you think of that?
    Meow, Meow

The song can also be sung going down the scale.

*Contributed by Carolyn Gardiner, North Kingstown, R.I.

## 5. REINFORCING SCIENTIFIC FACTS*

MATERIALS: Nothing special required.

PROCEDURE: Have the children rewrite the lyrics of a familiar song, such as "The Twelve Days of Christmas," following a scientific theme and staying within the category. For example:

### THE TWELVE DAYS OF SPRING

A blue robin's egg in a nest
Two yellow chicks
Three bunny rabbits
Four young colts
Five barking pups
Six mooing calves
Seven green tadpoles
Eight frisky kittens
Nine caterpillars
Ten leaping lambs
Eleven squealing pigs
Twelve singing crickets

This type of activity can be used for any scientific topic as well as for other curriculum areas.

*Contributed by Maureen Harrington, Westerly, R.I.

## 6. MAKING MUSICAL SOUNDS*

MATERIALS: Many and varied as noted for each of the projects described below.

PROCEDURE: The children are to make all their own instruments. Through construction, they become aware of the ways sound is made, the different kinds of sounds, what material makes sounds better than another material, and so forth.

*Conceived or collected by and contributed by Claudette Donnelly, Saunderstown, R.I., unless otherwise noted.

## Wind Instruments

MATERIALS: Various lengths of garden hose, funnel, mouthpiece.

PROCEDURE: Cut various lengths of garden hose. Tape a funnel to one end of each piece and a mouthpiece to the other end, and blow. The different lengths of hoses will produce different notes of the scale.

MATERIALS: A 12-inch length of hollow reed or bamboo, stiff wire, saw, ruler, ¾-inch length of twig, drill.

PROCEDURE: To make a toot flute, remove all the loose pith from the reed or bamboo with a piece of stiff wire. Make a saw cut 1½ inches from one end, just through to the hollow portion. Two and one-half inches from the same end, shave down the top of the reed to the bottom of the saw cut to give a thin-featured end. Cut a ¾-inch length of twig whose diameter is the same as the hole in the reed. Whittle a tapered plug so that the diameter of one end is ⅛ inch less than that of the hollow reed. Insert the plug with the whittled side matching the shaved side of the reed about ½ inch from the end of the reed. Drill five holes on the other end. Air is blown through the reed, and the plug is adjusted as to sound. Depending upon the ages of the students, they will most likely require help to make this flute.

## Drums

MATERIALS: Rags, pots and pans of different sizes, wooden and metal spoons.

PROCEDURE: Stuff rags into the different-size pots and pans. Hit the pans with wooden and metal spoons and other objects. Different sounds will be obtained (Strobell, 1975, pp. 107–10).

MATERIALS: Metal waste basket.

PROCEDURE: Hold the waste basket under one arm and tap on the bottom with the knuckles.

MATERIALS: Large cylindrical cartons, chamois.

PROCEDURE: Cut the top and bottom off of the carton. Cover the opening with tightly stretched chamois.

MATERIALS: Wooden chopping bowl, parchment.

PROCEDURE: Stretch the parchment tightly over the top of the chopping bowl. The result is a tom-tom.

MATERIALS: Metal canisters, such as used for flour and sugar.

PROCEDURE: Simply tap on the canisters, with the covers on. Coffee cans and large fruit juice cans can be used also.

### Triangle Substitutes

MATERIALS: Two large nails, string.

PROCEDURE: Suspend one of the large nails (use the largest nails available at the hardware store) from a short string. Strike the nail with the second one. Select nails carefully since some will produce almost no sound at all.

MATERIALS: Long eye bolts of various sizes, string, nail.

PROCEDURE: Attach the eye bolts to a string and suspend. Strike the bolts with a long nail.

### Stringed Instruments

MATERIALS: Chicken or turkey wishbone (or "Y"-shaped branch), rubber bands.

PROCEDURE: String one or more rubber bands across the opening. Put the wishbone on a table or in an empty can to change the sound (Strobell, 1975, pp. 107–10).

### Shakers

MATERIALS: Paper cups, pebbles, tape.

PROCEDURE: Put pebbles into one paper cup and then tape the cup to another paper cup, mouth to mouth, to make a rattle.

MATERIALS: Nuts and bolts, tea strainer; oil cloth, plastic, or chamois.

PROCEDURE: Put the nuts and bolts into the strainer and cover with the cloth.

MATERIALS: Plastic soap dish, baking powder can, plastic pill bottles, beans.

PROCEDURE: Put dried beans or other suitable objects into the container. Replace the lid, being certain it is tight. The pill bottles can be attached to an 8-inch stick, if desired.

MATERIALS: Plastic lemon and lime juice containers, shakeables, dowel stick.

PROCEDURE: Remove the pinhole cap from the plastic containers. Fill the bottles with shakeables and put a dowel stick into the opening to reseal the container.

## Knockers and Wood Block Substitutes

MATERIALS: Resonant wood, 8-inch by 10-inch thin boards, string, dowel stick.

PROCEDURE: Any hard, resonant wood, such as old chair legs, can be used to knock together. Or, holes can be drilled at the top of each of two thin boards so that strings can be inserted for holding. A dowel stick can be used for knocking the boards together.

## Scrapers

MATERIALS: Nails, wooden clothespins.

PROCEDURE: Nail a group of clothespins head down in a row. Scrape over the split part with a scraper.

MATERIALS: Metal thimbles, old washboard.

PROCEDURE: Place metal thimbles on two fingers and strum up and down on an old washboard.

## Tambourines

MATERIALS: Four heavy paper plates, laces, twelve bottle caps, string, paints.

PROCEDURE: Place the four plates one inside the other. Punch holes 1½ inches apart around the rim. Then put two plates face to face with the other two. Lace through the holes and tie. Punch holes in twelve bottle caps and string four to a group. Tie the four groups to the plates spacing them around the circumference. Paint or decorate with bright designs.

MATERIALS: Plastic lid from a coffee can, twelve bottle caps, string.

PROCEDURE: Punch two holes in the lid on opposite sides. Punch a hole in the center of each bottle cap. Thread string through the holes in half of the bottle caps and attach to one side of the lid. String the remaining caps in the same manner to the hole on the opposite side of the lid. The string should form a loop so that a piece from the bottom of the strung caps and a piece from the top of the strung caps are attached to the lid.

MATERIALS: Wire, five or six bottle caps, string.

PROCEDURE: Punch a hole in the center of each bottle cap. Attach them to a bent wire, like part of a coat hanger. Shaking them makes the sound.

MATERIALS: Soda bottle caps, dowel, nail.

PROCEDURE: Remove the cork from the bottle caps and flatten the caps. Two caps are then attached to an 8-inch long dowel by hammering a nail through them and into the dowel. Space must be left on the nail for the caps to shake. (See figure 5–9.)

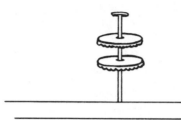

**Figure 5-9**

# Art Experiences and Related Games, Crafts, and Projects

### 1. UNDERSTANDING THE EARTH'S MOVEMENT

MATERIALS: Drawing paper.

PROCEDURE: Give the children an assignment to wake up early one morning and make a sketch to show the sun rising in relation to the trees and buildings. Then, every two or three hours, they are to observe the sun's position and make a sketch to show it. The finished products are put away for a month and then the project is repeated. When the entire activity is completed, all the pictures are taken out and compared and contrasted. A discussion should ensue about changes in the sun's position during one day and why they occur, and about seasonal changes and why they occur. The depth of the discussion will depend upon the level of the children.

### 2. LEARNING THE CONSTELLATIONS

MATERIALS: Dark blue paper, gummed silver stars.

PROCEDURE: Have the children place gummed silver stars on dark blue paper to represent various constellations. A game can then be played in which the children try to name the constellations made by the other children.

## 3. LEARNING THE SOLAR SYSTEM

MATERIALS: Three quarter-inch by 5-inch newsprint, ten balls ranging in size from Ping-Pong balls to a basketball, liquid glue, paints,
brushes, shellac, 4-inch lengths of glass tubing, eye screw, steel wire, turn
buckles, "s" hooks, cutting pliers, razor blades, petroleum jelly, flour,
water, aprons to protect the children.

PROCEDURE: To begin this group project, it is advisable for the
teacher to precut the wire so the children do not have to work with pliers.

a. Cover the balls with a thick coating of petroleum jelly.
b. Saturate the newsprint strips in flour paste and cover the balls.
   When they are dry, apply a coating of liquid glue. When the glue
   hardens, repeat the process five or six times. Plain and colored
   strips should be alternated.
c. Remove the ball by cutting around the circumference of the outer
   covering with a razor blade being careful not to damage the ball.
d. Join the hemispheres with two or more layers of saturated newsprint.
e. When dry, insert an eye screw into each sphere.
f. Paint each sphere completely with two or three coats of the desired
   colors. Lighten the same paint with some white and apply it to
   one-half of each sphere to represent the lighted portion of that
   planet. Allow some darker spots to show to represent the uneven
   surface of the planet.
g. Apply two or three coatings of shellac.
h. Moons are added by cementing one end of a piece of glass tubing
   to a Ping-Pong ball and the other to the sphere. The glass tubing
   should pierce the Ping-Pong ball and the sphere before the cement
   is applied. The moons may be painted gray or any desired color.
i. The different-size balls, from tennis to basketball, represent the
   different-size planets. The sun is the basketball.
j. The following table can be used to represent distances from the
   sun.

| Mercury | 1 inch | Saturn | 24 inches |
|---------|--------|--------|-----------|
| Venus | 2 inches | Uranus | 50 inches |
| Earth | 3 inches | Neptune | 76 inches |
| Mars | 4 inches | Pluto | 98 inches |
| Jupiter | 12 inches | | |

### 4. LEARNING THE CONSTELLATIONS

MATERIALS: Cardboard oatmeal carton, thin cardboard, scissors, flashlight.

PROCEDURE: To make a star theater, remove the lid of an oatmeal carton. Cut out the top of the lid to within ½ inch of the edge. Cut circles of thin cardboard to fit inside the lid of the carton. Each child should be given one of the circles to punch holes into to represent a constellation. There should be a hole punched for each star in the constellation. Different constellations should be assigned to students.

When the constellations are ready, cut off the bottom of the cardboard carton. Put a lighted flashlight in the bottom of the carton facing up toward the lid and insert the circle of cardboard with the constellation inside the lid. Place the lid on the carton. The constellation will now be projected on the ceiling of the darkened room. (See figure 5–10.)

To extend this activity, have the children read and discuss stories about characters for whom the stars and constellations were named.

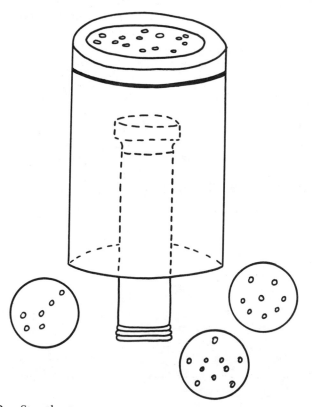

**Figure 5-10.**   Star theater.

## 5. RELATING NATURE TO MAN

MATERIALS: Drawing paper, camera, film, crayons, paint.

PROCEDURE: Have the children draw or photograph buildings or manmade objects. When they have done this, have them go outside and find something in nature that has the same shape. Then have them draw or photograph the thing in nature. The children share their pictures of something manmade and something in nature and explain how the shapes are the same. They compare and contrast their works and discuss what the other students have found (suggested by an activity in Kaplan et al., 1973, p. 37).

## 6. UNDERSTANDING POWER

MATERIALS: Drawing paper, camera, film, crayons, paint.

PROCEDURE: Have the children go outside and find things that represent power. They must then sketch, photograph, or paint the things. The artwork should depict the things in detail. The children exchange papers and discuss what kind of power is seen in the artwork of the others, how the power is used, when it is used, by whom it is used, and so forth.

## 7. LEARNING ABOUT FROST*

MATERIALS: Light blue and dark blue 9-inch by 12-inch construction paper, four strips of brown construction paper cut into 9-inch by 2-inch strips (two strips) and 12-inch by 1-inch strips (two strips), paintbrush, white tempera paint, paste, cellophane paper slightly larger than 9 inches by 12 inches.

PROCEDURE: The children are asked to design a windowpane frosted by ice or snow. The light blue paper is used for morning frost and the dark blue for evening frost. (See figure 5–11.)

a. Paint a lacy pattern on a piece of blue construction paper.

b. After the design has dried, paste cellophane over it.

c. Paste a frame around the design with brown construction paper to give it a windowpane look.

d. Several designs may be made and grouped together.

This activity can be followed with experiments to demonstrate the concept that, when warm moist air from indoors meets cool air from outdoors, water vapor is created and turns to water. The children can observe this happening on their windows at home when it is very cold outside. To demonstrate in the classroom, fill a glass with ice. Tiny beads of water will begin to appear on the outside of the glass. The water is not coming from inside the glass. Let the children discuss what is happening and figure out why.

*Contributed by Kathy McGregor, Narragansett, R.I.

**Figure 5-11**

## 8. SEEING ILLUSIONS

MATERIALS:  Drawing paper, pencils, crayons.

PROCEDURE:  Draw an illusion on the board such as is shown in figure 5–12. Discuss whether the lines appear to be the same size or different sizes. Have children come up and measure the lines to prove their actual lengths. Discuss instances in which things seem to be one thing and turn out to be different. Have the children suggest illusions they have seen or heard of. Then have them draw pictures of different kinds of illusions.

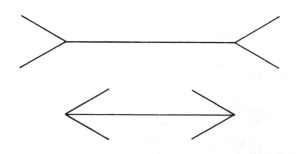

**Figure 5-12**

## 9. Learning About the Spectrum

Materials:  Stiff, round pieces of cardboard about 2½ to 3½ inches in diameter, paint, heavy string.

Procedure:  Have the children make color wheels.

a. Divide a cardboard circle into six sections and paint them the following colors, in order: red, orange, yellow, green, blue and violet.
b. Punch two holes a little apart at the center of the circle.
c. Take about 4 feet of heavy string, put it through the holes, and tie the ends.
d. To use the color wheel, center the circle on the string and, while holding the string loosely, wind it several times. Then quickly pull the string taut and relax it, which will start the wheel to spin. Repeat this several times. As the wheel spins faster, the children will see the colors blend together and become almost white.

This project should initiate a discussion of the spectrum and a study of color relationships.

## 10. Identifying Food Sources

Materials:  Cardboard pieces the size of playing cards, crayons, paint.

Procedure:  Distribute a pair of cards to each child. Tell the children they are to draw a food source on one card and write or draw the food on the other, for example, a cow and "milk." Check with the children to be certain there are no duplications. When the cards are completed, start a game in which each player gets four cards. (The children will have to be broken into groups. All groups will not be able to play at the same time unless the children make multiple pairs of the food and source cards.) After each player has four cards, the remainder are placed in a stack, face down. The first player asks for a corresponding card. If the player has a picture of a cow, then "milk" might be called for. If no one has "milk," the player draws from the pack. The winner is the child with the most pairs. This game can also be played like Concentration (Kaplan et al., 1973, p. 45).

## 11. Understanding Scientific Development

Materials:  Drawing paper, crayons, paint.

Procedure:  Have the children trace the development of an invention, such as the airplane, the car, the telephone. The children then draw pictures to represent the changes in the invention over a period of time and write a summary to describe the changes. They may also find existing pictures of the item and include them in their reports. The topics can be extended to such things as power sources and architecture.

## 12. RECOGNIZING STIMULI FOR INVENTIONS

MATERIALS: Newspaper.
PROCEDURE: Present the group with a problem: "We all need hats for our show, and all we have are sheets of newspaper and no scissors. What can we do?" Let the children experiment until they see that the newspaper can be folded into a hat, can be stapled and pasted. Ask the children to think of other situations in which things can be used in different ways. Guide the discussion to inventions: why they came about, why they are important, and so forth.

## 13. NOTING DESIGNS

MATERIALS: Drawing paper, crayons, paint, camera, film.
PROCEDURE: Have the children look for designs in nature that start from a center point. The children should keep a log of drawings, paintings, and photographs based on observation. In addition, the children are asked to look for pictures of things in nature that start from a center point. These pictures are added to their logs. The students should begin to see different kinds of designs, including radial designs seen in flowers, shells, and some fruits and vegetables and spiral designs seen in ferns, some animal horns, and certain types of shells. After many observations, the students can create their own designs (Cooke, 1973, pp. 12, 13).

## 14. FOLLOWING SCIENTIFIC PROCEDURE

MATERIALS: Camera, film, drawing paper, crayons, paints.
PROCEDURE: Have the children photograph the step-by-step process of a scientific experiment and add captions describing the procedure and results (Waller, 1981, p. 94). Or, the children can make illustrations of the experiments and add captions to describe the procedure and results.

## 15. OBSERVING NATURE

MATERIALS: Camera and Film.
PROCEDURE: Take the children on a field trip to view something specific in nature. Photograph the items observed. The photos are put together, and science stories are written based on what was seen and represented in the photographs (Waller, 1981, p. 94).

## 16. LEARNING ABOUT AERODYNAMICS

MATERIALS: Kite-building materials.

PROCEDURE: Have each child build a kite and try to fly it. The children should not be shown how to do this. The children should then compare which kite flew the longest, the highest, the fastest. They should note which kites would not fly at all. Then they should try to determine why each of the above happened. Based on their observations, the children try to redesign their kites so they will fly better. The children can do some research to help them and to learn more about the subject.

## 17. REFERENCES

NEWNHAM, JACK. *Kites to Make and Fly*, 1978. This book describes in detail how to make and fly four different kites: a flat kite with a tail, a bowed kite without a tail, a box kite, and a lightweight "stunt" kite. All four kites are made with simple materials and simple tools. The directions are complete and easy to follow.

# Drama Experiences and Related Games, Crafts, and Projects

## 1. RECOGNIZING SEQUENCE IN NATURE

MATERIALS: Nothing special required.

PROCEDURE: Divide the children into groups. Working together, each group acts out a sequential action, such as the earth moving around the sun or the moon moving around the earth. The remaining children try to determine what sequence is being portrayed. They should discuss the accuracies and inaccuracies in the performance.

## 2. DISCOVERING ACTION-REACTION

MATERIALS: Nothing special required.

PROCEDURE: Divide the children into pairs. One person in each pair makes a movement or sound that requires a response from the partner. The partner responds and starts a new activity that requires its own response. Each child should work with a few partners before the entire group comes together to share experiences and to discuss which movements call for a response, which do not, and why. The discussion should then be related to the concepts of action-reaction. Provide examples and have the children discuss these and suggest other examples (King, 1975, p. 262).

## 3. Imitating Things in Nature

MATERIALS: Nothing special required.

PROCEDURE: Have the children make a list of items found outdoors that move. When the lists are complete, the children try to move as those items do. The other children try to determine what thing is being imitated. Many things move: leaves blowing, worms crawling, birds flying, buds opening. This activity makes the children more aware of movements taking place, many of which they never thought about before.

## 4. Demonstrating Laws of Motion

MATERIALS: Nothing special required.

PROCEDURE: Establish a point on the floor at one end of the room. Have the children take turns running, trotting, walking, hopping, and so forth, stopping just before the mark. Lead them to see that it takes longer to stop when they are going faster. Discuss why. Ask for other examples, and discuss why longer runways are needed for some planes and so forth. Through this activity, the children should see that an object in motion tends to remain in motion (King, 1975, p. 132).

## 5. Learning About Physical Changes

MATERIALS: Sheet of paper.

PROCEDURE: Discuss physical changes: that an object may change in one way or another but retain its original properties. Demonstrate by tearing or cutting a sheet of paper into two or more pieces, so the children can see that the size and shape have changed but the paper is still paper. Then put the pieces back together so that the original is restored. When this is completed and has been discussed, ask the children to pretend they are snow statues. On a signal they are to freeze. On another signal the sun comes out and they are to begin to melt. On a third signal they are to freeze again into a different shape based on where they were in the thawing process. Keep repeating the freezing and thawing process. Two or more statutes might melt together to make a larger statue. Experiment with fast and slow thaws and discuss each of these in detail (King, 1975, p. 117).

# REFERENCES

CLARK, ELIZABETH. "The Seed That Grew." *The Instructor* (March 1961): 60.

COOKE, R. "Photography and Visual Awareness." *School Arts* (September 1973): 12–13.

DAVIS, BETTE. *Insects That Make Musical Sounds.* New York: Lothrop, Lee and Shepard Co., 1971.

JANIAK, WILLIAM. *Developing Everyday Skills* and *Songs About Me.* Long Branch, N.J.: Kimbo Educational. Records.

KAPLAN, SANDRA NINA; KAPLAN, JO ANN BUTOM; MADSEN, SHEILA KUMISHIMA; AND TAYLOR, BETTE K. *Change for Children.* Santa Monica: Goodyear Publishing Co., 1973.

KING, NANCY. *Giving Form to Feeling.* New York: Drama Book Specialists/Publishers, 1975.

MANN, BARBARA FAY. *Food Fun Songbook.* 1805 Aisquith Road, Richmond, VA. 23229, 1973.

NEWNHAM, JACK. *Kites to Make and Fly.* Victoria, Australia: Penguin Books Australia Ltd., 1978.

REYNOLDS, MALVINA. *Little Boxes and Other Handmade Songs.* New York: Oak Publications, 1964.

STROBELL, ADAH PARKER. *Bicentennial Games 'N Fun.* Washington, D.C.: Acropolis Books, 1975.

TAYLOR, FRANK D., ARTUSO, ALFRED A., AND HEWETT, FRANK M. *Creative Art Tasks for Children.* Denver: Love Publishing Co., 1970.

WALLER, VICTORIA MILLER. "Lights, Camera, Action! The Camera as a Tool for Teaching Reading." In *Motivating Reluctant Readers,* edited by Alfred J. Ciani. Newark, Del.: International Reading Association, 1981.

# CHAPTER 6

# *Mathematics Experiences*

THE EXPERIENCES IN THIS CHAPTER are presented in two broad areas: basic facts and general topics.

## BASIC FACTS

Learning basic facts is absolutely necessary to the development of mathematics skills. In this section, experiences are suggested to assist in the development of the basic areas of numbers, computation, measurement, proportions, and fractions.

### Music Experiences and Related Games, Crafts, and Projects

1. PRACTICING NUMBER KNOWLEDGE*

MATERIALS: Nothing special required.

PROCEDURE: Teach the rhythm game "Who Stole the Cookie?" The children all chant, "Who stole the cookie from the cookie jar?" The first child selects a number and chants, "Number 5 [or any other number] stole the cookie from the cookie jar." The child whose number was called chants, "Who me?" The leader chants in response, "Yes, you." The child whose number was called chants, "Couldn't be." The leader chants, "Then who?" The child whose number was called selects another number and chants, "Number 19 [or any other number] stole the cookie from the cookie jar."

The game continues with the conversation between the new leader and the child whose number has now been called. As each number is called, the teacher crosses the number off the board so it won't be repeated.

Who Stole the Cookie?

3 5 7 9 11 13 15 17 19

The chant is done in four-quarter time by having the children snap their fingers and clap alternately. Each child is secretly assigned one of the possible answer numbers. In this way, no one knows until the end of the game who the thief is.

To vary the game and make it more difficult, the numbers are not written on the board beforehand. The children are told simply that all the numbers are odd, or all are even, and so forth. The numbers are written on the board after they are called. This game is good to use for random numbers, even and odd, multiples, division, fractions, decimals, and Roman numerals.

*Contributed by Maureen Harrington, Westerly, R.I.

## 2. Solving Problems*

Materials: Cards with number problems.

Procedure: Teach the children the following words to the melody of "Mary Had a Little Lamb."

I see someone with a _____[any number]
With a _____, with a _____
I see someone with a _____
"Stand up" if you have _____

Give the children number-card stories, such as 3 +1 =, and have the child stand up when the number called is the answer to the problem held by the child. The children take turns being the leader and singing a number. The directions can be varied so that the child with the answer to the problem has to do different things instead of standing up. Such things could be to hop, wave, or jump. This game can be used also for vocabulary development, for colors, for letter identification, and so forth.

*Contributed by Nora Safford, Charlestown, R.I.

### 3. Practicing Computation*

MATERIALS: Mathematical equations or problems.

PROCEDURE: A number of melodies, familiar to the children, are determined. Then a number of mathematical equations or problems, at a level of difficulty appropriate to the group, are set up. Each problem should have an answer that works out to a number from one to ten plus halves. Multiple-choice answers can be used.

The notes for one and one-half octaves of the scale, or two octaves, are each assigned a number:

| middle | | high | |
|---|---|---|---|
| C=1 | C#=$1\frac{1}{2}$ | C=8 | C#=$8\frac{1}{2}$ |
| D=2 | D#=$2\frac{1}{2}$ | D=9 | D#=$9\frac{1}{2}$ |
| E=3 | E#=$3\frac{1}{2}$ | E=10 | E#=$10\frac{1}{2}$ |
| F=4 | F#=$4\frac{1}{2}$ | | |
| G=5 | G#=$5\frac{1}{2}$ | | |
| A=6 | A#=$6\frac{1}{2}$ | | |
| B=7 | B#=$7\frac{1}{2}$ | | |

A worksheet is then prepared, as shown below. The time must be marked.

Problem 1: $\frac{4}{4}$ time

Note 1:   $2000 \div 2 \div 4 \div 2 + 5 \div 2 - 59 \qquad = \underline{\quad 6 \quad}$

Note 2:   $\frac{1}{2} + 3 + 1 - \frac{1}{2} + 5 - 3\frac{1}{2} \qquad\qquad = \underline{\quad 5\frac{1}{2} \quad}$

Note 3:   $1{,}000{,}000 - 100{,}000 + 2 - 899{,}999 - 1\frac{1}{2} = \underline{\quad 1\frac{1}{2} \quad}$

And so forth. A sufficient number of bars should be included so that the pupils can discern the melody. The answer to the problem begun above is shown in figure 6–1.

The worksheets should be passed out and the students given sufficient time to solve the problems. Then the students are asked to put their

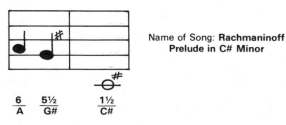

Name of Song: **Rachmaninoff
Prelude in C# Minor**

$\dfrac{6}{A}$   $\dfrac{5\frac{1}{2}}{G\#}$   $\dfrac{1\frac{1}{2}}{C\#}$

**Figure 6-1**

answers on the board in order. When the correct answers are determined, the students transpose the answers onto worksheets containing the lines of the staff. To check accuracy of the answers, the music can then be played on various instruments. An extension to this would have the pupils making up their own math problems with answers that create a song. If some pupils cannot play an instrument, the numbers can be taped on the keys of a toy piano, organ, and so forth, so that the students will be able to play the numbers in the answer. This experience is designed for the upper elementary grades.

## Sample Worksheets for Musical Mathematics

a.　Note 1:　$4 - 1 + 5 - 2 + 3$　　　　　$=$ _____
　　Note 2:　$1\frac{1}{2} + 9 - 2 + 1 - 1$　　　　$=$ _____
　　Note 3:　$7 + 4 + 1 - 5 + 0$　　　　$=$ _____
　　Note 4:　$8 + 9 - 7 - 4 + 0$　　　　$=$ _____
　　Note 5:　$0 + 9 \times 3 - 22$　　　　　$=$ _____
　　Note 6:　$8 \mid \frac{1}{2} + \frac{1}{2} + \frac{1}{2} - 5$　　　$=$ _____
　　Note 7:　$\frac{1}{2} \div \frac{1}{4} \div \frac{1}{4} + 2$　　　　$=$ _____
　　Note 8:　$1 \times 1 \times 1 \times 1 + 1$　　　$=$ _____
　　$\frac{2}{4}$ time　　　　　　　　　Song Title:_____
　　(See figure 6–2.)

**Figure 6-2**

b.　Note 1:　$8 - 3 \times 5 - 20$　　　　　$=$ _____
　　Note 2:　$\frac{1}{2} + \frac{1}{2} \times 5 \times 2$　　　　$=$ _____
　　Note 3:　$8 - 3 \times 2 - 1$　　　　　$=$ _____
　　Note 4:　$\frac{1}{2} \times 4 \times 4 + 0$　　　　$=$ _____
　　Note 5:　$\frac{1}{4} + \frac{1}{4} \times 18$　　　　　$=$ _____
　　Note 6:　$7 \times 2 - 4 - 2$　　　　　$=$ _____
　　Note 7:　$3 \times 3 - 3 + 0$　　　　　$=$ _____
　　Note 8:　$18 - 15 + 2$　　　　　　$=$ _____
　　Note 9:　$90 - 80 - 7$　　　　　　$=$ _____
　　$\frac{3}{4}$ time　　　　　　　　　Song Title:_____
　　(See figure 6–3.)

**Figure 6-3**

c.  Note 1:  $\frac{1}{2} + \frac{1}{2} + \frac{1}{2} + 2 + 1$     = \_\_\_\_\_
    Note 2:  $38 - 33 - 2$     = \_\_\_\_\_
    Note 3:  $8 - 2 - 2 - 2$     = \_\_\_\_\_
    Note 4:  $10 - 4 - 2 - 2$     = \_\_\_\_\_
    Note 5:  same as #1     = \_\_\_\_\_
    Note 6:  same as #2     = \_\_\_\_\_
    Note 7:  same as #3     = \_\_\_\_\_
    Note 8:  same as #4     = \_\_\_\_\_
    $\frac{6}{8}$ time     Song Title:_____
    (See figure 6–4.)

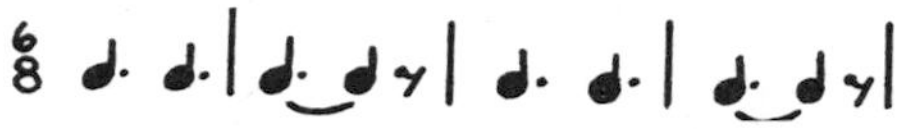

**Figure 6-4**

d.  Note 1:  $2 + 1 - 1 + 3$     = \_\_\_\_\_
    Note 2:  $10 \times 2 - 10 - 5$     = \_\_\_\_\_
    Note 3:  $18 - 5 - 4 + 0$     = \_\_\_\_\_
    Note 4:  $2\frac{1}{2} + 2\frac{1}{2} + 4$     = \_\_\_\_\_
    Note 5:  $40 - 20 - 10$     = \_\_\_\_\_
    Note 6:  $50 - 30 - 10$     = \_\_\_\_\_
    Note 7:  same as #4     = \_\_\_\_\_
    $\frac{2}{4}$ time     Song Title:_____
    (See figure 6–5.)

**Figure 6-5**

The answers for some typical songs are shown in figure 6–6.

*Contributed by Roberta M. Humble, Associate Professor of English, Rhode Island Junior College.

### 4. Measuring Time

**Materials:** Stopwatch, recorded music.

**Procedure:** Have the children time various musical selections, movements, and so forth, and compare and contrast the results. A fun thing to do is to have them time "The Minute Waltz." They may also time popular LP recordings or measure the amount of time spent playing music during a half-hour television show.

Figure 6-6

## 5. UNDERSTANDING FRACTIONAL RELATIONSHIPS

MATERIALS: A large floor area, chalk, recorded music.

PROCEDURE: Divide the children into four groups, each representing a different fraction: eighths, fourths, halves, and the whole. Clear a floor area and draw lines indicating a start position, a finish position, one-fourth the distance, and one-half the distance. Explain that, as the music plays, the eighths will take eight small steps to reach the next line, the fourths will take four steps to reach it, the halves will take two steps, and the wholes will take one step. At first, have each group walk individually to the beat. Then have two walk together, then three, then four, until everyone understands what is to be done and has mastered the rhythm. Discuss the fact that they all wind up in the same place at the same time, despite the number of steps taken. Liken the fractions to musical notes of the same values. The activity can be begun with a clapping rhythm and then progress to the playing of music. The activity should reinforce the relationship among the fractions (King, 1975, p. 276). (See figure 6–7.)

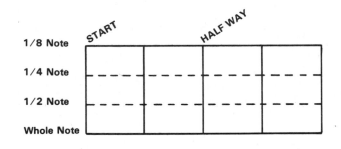

**Figure 6-7**

## 6. ADDING FRACTIONS

MATERIALS:  Copies of sheet music written in four-quarter time.

PROCEDURE:  Hand out the sheet music. Ask the children to add the fractional values of each note in a bar and get a total for each bar. In four-quarter time the bars will all add up to 1. When the children are more proficient, use music written in different times. The bars will not add up to 1, but each bar will add up to the same amount. Be careful not to use music with rests included unless these have been taught.

## 7. RECOGNIZING QUARTER AND HALF NOTES

MATERIALS:  Written-out patterns of music.

PROCEDURE:  Teach the children what a quarter note and a half note look like (figure 6–8). Write out a pattern of music and have the children clap hands to the beat; half notes are held for two beats (a half note is the same length as two quarter notes). Start with repeating patterns, as in example A, and then vary the patterns, as in example B. Become more complex as the children are ready by adding eighth and sixteenth notes (figure 6–9).

**Figure 6-8**

Example A: ♩♪♪ ♩♪♪

Example B: ♪♪♩ ♪♪♪♪ ♩♪♪

**Figure 6-9**

## 8. SINGING MATHEMATICS

MATERIALS: Math songs.

PROCEDURE: Teach some of the well-known songs that can be used for counting, multiplication, and so forth: "Ten Little Indians," "This Old Man," "One, Two, Button My Shoe," "One Potato, Two Potato," "John Brown Had a Little Indian," "Weevily Wheat."

## 9. SINGING ADDITION*

MATERIALS: Nothing special required.

PROCEDURE: Using the tune of "Twinkle Twinkle," teach the following song. The + marks are pronounced as *plus*.

> Adding, adding, let's begin
> 3 + 3 + 4 is 10.
> Add three numbers, make them rhyme,
> 3 + 3 + 3 is nine.
> *(Repeat first two lines)*
> Adding, adding, this is great,
> 4 + 3 + 1 is 8.
> Add three numbers, get to heaven,
> 4 + 2 + 1 is 7.
> *(Repeat fifth and sixth lines)*
> Adding, adding, numbers mix,
> 1 + 2 + 3 is 6.
> Add three numbers, come alive,
> 1 + 2 + 2 is 5.
> *(Repeat ninth and tenth lines)*
> Adding, adding think some more,
> 1 + 1 + 2 is 4.
> Add three numbers, sing with me,
> 1 + 1 + 1 is 3.
> *(Repeat thirteenth and fourteenth lines)*
> Adding, adding, tell me true,
> 1 + 1 + 0 is 2.
> Add three numbers, this is fun,
> 1 + 0 + 0 is 1,
> Now our song is really done,
> 0 + 0 + 0 is none.

After the children have learned the song, have them fill in their own numbers to total each product. Then, sitting in a circle, each child sings two lines until all have had a turn. When a product is repeated, the three numbers should be different, that is, 3 + 3 + 4 and 1 + 5 + 4.

*Contributed by Patty Dickens, Reno, Nevada.

## 10. Translating Note Patterns*

Materials: A piano or xylophone.

Procedure: Demonstrate how 2 + 2 + 1 = 5 can be translated musically into "CC GG E", for instance. Play or sing the pattern to the students. Then have the children echo the pattern orally. The next step is to have the students write down the equation for the pattern. Thus, C D EE G would be written as 1 + 1 + 2 + 1 = 5; AAA GG E would be 3 + 2 + 1 = 6, and so forth. An attempt should be made to try to incorporate a rhythm as the notes are played. For example, C FFF (1 + 3) is the beginning of "Here Comes the Bride."

*Contributed by Janice (J. J.) McIntosh, Port Orchard, Washington.

## 11. Adding Fractions*

Materials: Notation problems.

Procedure: After the students have been taught how to read notes and the values of notes, they can be given addition, subtraction, multiplication, and division problems using notation. Examples of some addition and subtraction problems are shown in figure 6–10.

*Contributed by Krista Bottyan, Delta, British Columbia.

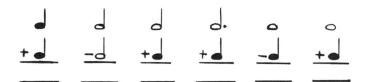

**Figure 6-10**
*Illustration by Lewis S. List*

## 12. References

Palmer, Hap. (volume I, #AR514). This record includes a game called "The Number March." The children march around a circle to music. They begin by adding one person at a time and counting the total each time. Then they subtract one person at a time and note the number left.

Volume 2, #AR522 presents a "Lucky Numbers" game. Number cards from

1 to 20 are placed on the edge of a circle. The children march around the circle until a bell rings. At that time, they run to stand beside one of the numbers. When the child's number is called, the child raises a hand. Then a number wheel is spun and one child is the lucky number winner.

Palmer also has an album on *Math Readiness* (#AR541) and *Sing Multiplication Tables* (#45–101). The multiplication materials cover 1 through 12 and are available only on record. The readiness material comes in cassette tape or record form.

JANIAK, WILLIAM. *Developing Everyday Skills* (#7016) and *Songs About Me* (#7022). These albums include mathematics activities.

REICHARD, CARY L., AND BLACKBURN, DENNIS B. (1973) Activities 24 through 55 are devoted to arithmetic.


# Art Experiences and Related Games, Crafts, and Projects


## 1. PRACTICING COMPUTATION

MATERIALS: A worksheet of a clown or other figure with number problems written in, as shown in figure 6–11.

PROCEDURE: Give the children the worksheet along with a key for a number-color relationship. For example:

5 = red
7 = green
8 = yellow
9 = blue

The number problems must be appropriate for the child or the group. The children are asked to solve each of the problems and then to color the spaces with the color indicated by the answer to the problem. As an extension, the children can make up their own pictures, problems, and code.


## 2. ILLUSTRATING COMPUTATIONS*

MATERIALS: Drawing paper

PROCEDURE: Have the children draw pictures to illustrate the answers to mathematics problems. For example,

a. Using balls, show $3 + 2 = 5$.
b. Using pencils, show $2 + 4 = 6$.
c. Using books, show $7 - 3 = 4$.
d. Using apples, show $6 - 3 = 3$.

**Figure 6-11**

The children can also be given problems without the answers. The problems should be appropriate to the level of the children. The children must first solve the problems and then illustrate them and the answer. (See figure 6–12.)

*Contributed by Carolyn Gardiner, North Kingstown, R.I.

### 3. Measuring

Materials: Construction paper, rulers, scissors, tape, staples, decorating materials.

Procedure: In conjunction with a class play or other activity, have the children make their own costumes. Each child measures another for

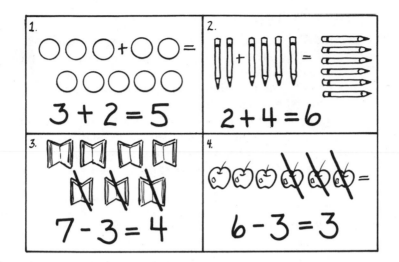

**Figure 6-12**

the length of the costume. Construction paper is unrolled to twice the desired length plus 12 additional inches. The children do all the measuring. The paper is folded in half at the shoulders. Each child cuts a neck hole large enough for the head to go through and then decorates the costume. When it is put on, the sides are attached with tape or staples (Kranz and Deley, 1970, pp. 87, 88).

### 4. ESTIMATING MEASUREMENT

MATERIALS: Drawing paper.

PROCEDURE: Ask the children to find something that is a million or more, and prove it and draw it. They might suggest there are more than a million bricks in a tall building. To prove it, they would measure how many bricks there are to each 5-foot-square area and then multiply by the length and the estimated height of the building. Or, they can be asked to count something they can't see and then draw it. A discussion should follow on how it could be measured. The finished works of the children should be shared and discussed. Other children may have different ideas for how a million or more can be proven, errors may be found in the computations, and so forth.

### 5. USING METRICS

MATERIALS: Drawing paper.

PROCEDURE: Have the children draw human figures or animals using metric measurements as their proportional guides.

### 6. Measuring Ingredients

MATERIALS: Varied, according to the item being measured.

PROCEDURE: Have the children mix paints and make paste by measuring the amounts needed of each ingredient. To make salt paste: Add two parts salt to one part flour. Add powdered paint and mix to a smooth consistency. Or, finger paint: Mix one cup laundry starch with one cup cold water. Add four cups of boiling water and cook until clear while stirring. Or, play dough: Mix three cups flour with one-fourth cup salt. Add one cup of water, with food coloring, and one tablespoon of oil gradually. These recipes and many more can be found in Croft and Hess (1972, pp. 85–88).

### 7. Reinforcing Number Meaning

MATERIALS: Magazines.

PROCEDURE: Have the children look through magazines and cut out pictures that show "one" of something, "two," "three," and so forth. These pictures are then pasted onto a large piece of paper to represent pictures of the numbers.

### 8. Practicing Numbering*

MATERIALS: Finger paint, art paper.

PROCEDURE: Ask the children to think of a simple picture they can draw, such as a fish or a clown face. Then have the children dip their fingers into finger paint and make dabs to make an outline of the items they thought of. Spaces should be left between the dabs. When they are finished, they should number the dabs so that, if the numbers are followed, the picture will be complete. The papers are then exchanged and the numbered dabs are connected to make a picture. Children should discuss the results since the numbers may be in the wrong order or the wrong position. The child who completes the picture has to be able to tell what it is. (See figure 6–13.)

*Contributed by Kathy McGregor, Narragansett, R.I.

### 9. Reinforcing Number Meaning

MATERIALS: Large sheets of paper, crayons, paste.

PROCEDURE: Have the children divide a large sheet into boxes. In the first box they draw or paste a picture of one thing, in the second box two things, and so forth. Or, they draw the number of things indicated by a number prewritten into each box.

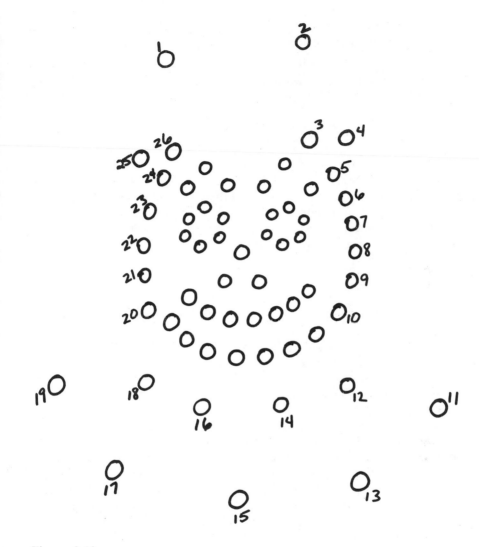

**Figure 6-13**

## 10. UNDERSTANDING ORDINALS*

MATERIALS: Copies of a picture with many items in it, crayons.

PROCEDURE: Supply pictures to the children, such as a clown holding ten balloons, a tree with ten birds sitting in a row, a fence with ten cats sitting on it. Then give directions such as "Color the first balloon green" or "Color the third balloon blue." Or, "Put an orange x on the second balloon," "Put a blue square around the fifth balloon." Use a different color, mark, or shape for each ordinal.

*Contributed by Claudette Donnelly, Saunderstown, R.I.
A reverse procedure can also be used; that is, instruct the children to draw a picture in which the first, third, and seventh items are blue, and so forth.

## 11. MEASURING TO SCALE

MATERIALS: Graph paper, rulers.
PROCEDURE: Have the children draw things to scale. They could make a scale drawing of some room in their house, the classroom, or the path from home to school. The children must decide what scale to use. Their decisions should be based on the size of the items to be reduced as well as the size of the paper the reproduction will go on.

## 12. ESTIMATING*

MATERIALS: Items made of silver and silver plate, play money, chocolate kisses.
PROCEDURE: Have the children bring in items made of silver or silver plate. Pictures of silver items can be used but they are not as effective as the actual items. Items that are no longer in use or are rarely seen are particular good to include so that a discussion of the item's function can take place.

Present some well-known quotations that contain the word "silver," for example, "Every man was not born with a silver spoon in his mouth," and "There's a silver lining through the dark clouds shining." Ask the children what these phrases mean. Develop the positive aspects of silver. Then explain and give a brief history of silver and silver making. Discuss the differences between silver and silver plate. Introduce the different variation and styles, such as vermeil and gold wash, engraved and repoused, monogrammed. During the discussion, introduce weight and troy ounces. Explain how troy ounces are determined.

Set up a game. Each student is given the same amount of play money. An auction is started using the following rules.

a. Each item will be auctioned. The prize will not be the item itself.
b. No child can spend more money than is given to the child.
c. The object of the game is to bid the closest to the market value of the item being auctioned without going over the market value.
d. The one who comes closest will receive a prize in chocolate kisses. The number of chocolates in the prize bag is unknown.
e. In order to determine how high to bid, the children must estimate

the value of the items during the preauction examination time. They may weigh the items, determine the value by the current price of an ounce of silver, and so forth.

f. When the auction is over, the children may spend any leftover money by trading the dollars for candy kisses as follows:

$100 = 4 kisses
  50 = 3 kisses
  20 = 2 kisses
  10 = 1 kiss
   1 = 0 kisses

Many lessons can be learned in this activity. Children learn how to be responsible for their own money, how to figure their money mathematically, how to make a decision (a bird in hand . . .?); they realize the value of silver and the value of money; and they gain some insight into risk. This lesson can also be used in science.

*Contributed by Roberta M. Humble, Associate Professor of English, Rhode Island Junior College.

## 13. MEASURING

MATERIALS: Construction paper, narrow strips of paper, scissors, rulers, dice, paste, crayons, paint.

PROCEDURE: Have each child make a head that looks like a worm's (figure 6–14). Each child also gets narrow strips of paper. In preparation for the game, the teacher covers one die on all sides with fractions. The children then roll both the dice and measure a strip of paper to the fraction rolled (See figure 6–15.) The first child to make a 20-inch worm

**Figure 6-14**

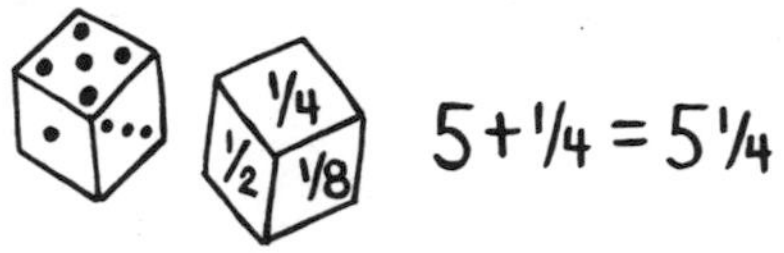

$$5 + 1/4 = 5\,1/4$$

**Figure 6-15**

wins. The children then color or paint their worms (Kaplan et al., 1973, p. 70).

## 14. MIXING MEASUREMENTS

MATERIALS: Various-colored paints, brushes, art paper.

PROCEDURE: The children are taught that few colors are pure, that is, things that are red are not all red, items that are blue are not all blue, and so forth. They are taught that colors must be mixed in order to approximate true colors. A daffodil might be 90 percent white, 10 percent cardinal yellow, and a touch of cardinal deep yellow; a carrot can be 85 percent white, 15 percent medium cardinal yellow, and a touch of burnt umber. The children should experiment with paint proportions to get more natural colors. They should record the proportions with which they experiment for each item and note the colors and proportions finally determined.

A game can be made out of this. An item, such as a pear, can be displayed and the children instructed to mix paints until they find the proportions that will result in the most natural colors. The final results can be compared and contrasted and one or more children can be deemed the winners.

## 15. USING MEASUREMENT INSTRUMENTS*

MATERIALS: Compass, ruler, sharp pencil, wallpaper scraps, fabric scraps, felt scraps, corrugated paper, drawing paper, paints, felt-tip pens, scissors, white glue or paste.

PROCEDURE: Explain to the children that they are going to make animals using the compass and the ruler. The head, body, curved ears, tails, and arms will be made with the compass. The legs, pointed ears, and pointed tails, will be made with the ruler. The children must first experiment with the compass to determine the size of the head and body, remembering that the head should be smaller than the body. The children write down the numbers used for each part of the body and the ruler measurements used for each section measured. They make a key so that they can remember all the measurements determined. The animal can be made from one or more of the art materials available and pasted onto a sheet of paper. Backgrounds can be painted. Or, the animal can be drawn onto a sheet of paper and then painted. Figure 6–16 shows a bear made entirely with a compass.

*Contributed by Eileen Rasmussen, Sparks, Nevada.

**Figure 6-16**
*Illustration by Eileen Rasmussen*

## 16. Reference

Wechemeyer, Avaril, and Cejka, Joyce (1979, #7511). These authors have developed *Color by Number* spirit masters. Each number corresponds with a specific color and each space in the picture is numbered.

# Drama Experiences and Related Games, Crafts, and Projects

## 1. Demonstrating Concepts

Materials:  Nothing special required.
Procedure:  Have the children make up a game in which they use movement to demonstrate the concept of adding or subtracting or multiplying or dividing. A group can be established to demonstrate the concept, and the remaining children try to determine what concept is being

illustrated. The group might set up a counting game in which they add one person at a time, and so forth. Music may be played as a background or to set the rhythm for the game.

## 2. Reinforcing Counting

MATERIALS: Nothing special required.

PROCEDURE: Break a group of children into two teams. Team 1 is directed to speak and clap on the letters. Team 2 is to answer and clap on the numbers. While team 1 speaks and claps, team 2 snaps to the beat. While team 2 speaks and claps, team 1 snaps to the beat.

|  | clap |  | clap |  |
|---|---|---|---|---|
| Team 1: | ABCD | snap | EFGH | snap |
| Team 2: | snap | 26, 25, 24, 23 | snap | 22, 21, 20, 19 |
|  |  | clap |  | clap |

An extension of this activity involves having each team walk forward four steps with the four claps and backward four steps with the snaps. Or, both teams do both parts, walking forward and clapping on the letters and backward and snapping on the numbers (Nash et al, 1977, p. 72).

## 3. Understanding Fractional Relationships

MATERIALS: A large floor area.

PROCEDURE: Get a group of four children. Assign one to be the eighth note, one the quarter note, one the half note, and one the whole note. The group will work in a unit of four measures. Using the same basic quarter note as the beat, the person who is the eighth note will clap thirty-two times, the quarter note will clap sixteen times, the half note will clap eight times, and the whole note will clap four times. Everyone starts on the first count of each measure. After the clapping is understood, walk through the rhythms according to the diagram (figure 6–17). D is the pivot person, who changes direction but remains in the same place, at the center. To make sure no one gets ahead, have the four children tap the rhythms with their feet. If groups of children act as each note, then have each group hold hands and tap the rhythms with their feet.

Discuss the relationship of the fractions. Children with severe math problems should remain as the whole-note part. The shape may be changed from a circle to anything else. This is a difficult activity and should be taught slowly. Have the children discuss the problems encountered (King, 1975, pp. 277, 278).

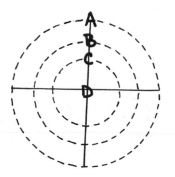

**Figure 6-17**

### 4. PRACTICING FACTS

MATERIALS: Flash cards.

PROCEDURE: Pass out addition, subtraction, multiplication, and division cards. Each child gets a problem, such as 7 + 2 =, or 6 × 7 =. Establish a rhythm to which all clap. The cards are displayed so that every child in the group can see each card. Select one child to begin. Then, in order and to the beat, each child calls out the correct answer to his or her problem.

### 5. PRACTICING MULTIPLICATION

MATERIALS: A drum.

PROCEDURE: The children form a circle. Beginning with child number 1, each student calls out a number and passes the drum. On the number 5 or any multiple of 5, or any other multiplication table sequence desired, the child hits the drum instead of speaking. If an error is made, the child goes into the center of the circle and must call an error to get back into the circle by exchanging places with the student who missed. The goal is to reach the number 100 without an error. After each mistake, the game begins again with number 1 (Nash et al., 1977, p. 66).

## GENERAL TOPICS

Included in this section are experiences for symmetry, direction, graphs, shapes, and time.

## Music Experiences and Related Games, Crafts, and Projects

### 1. OBSERVING SYMMETRY

MATERIALS: A filmed, televised, or live dance performance.

PROCEDURE: Have the students watch a dance production and note the symmetry of the group and the symmetrical patterns formed by individuals in the group. A ballet is particularly good for this as are some of the dance production numbers on television specials. Frequently, the dancers are viewed from above by the camera and the symmetrical movements of the group are easy to discern. Discuss the symmetry noted by the children, when it occurred, how it occurred, and what was involved in achieving it.

### 2. ALLOCATING TIME

MATERIALS: Nothing special required.

PROCEDURE: Have each child plan a sixty-minute musical program. Each child's program, though, will begin at a different time. One child will plan for 2:07 to 3:07, another for 1:37 to 2:37, and so forth. Instruct the children that every fifteen minutes, on the quarter hour, there must be a one-minute break between songs. Have them select a group of records they would like to play and time each. Then they should arrange the selections so that an entire hour is consumed and the songs end on the quarter hour. If the children are not mature enough, round off the seconds required for a record to the nearest whole minute. Older children should be able to add the seconds as well as the minutes. This activity can be simplified by eliminating the break times.

### 3. REFERENCES

PALMER, HAP. "Paper Clocks" (volume 2, #AR522). A song that directs the children to move the hands on their paper clocks to specific times named.

————. *Math Readiness* (#AR540). An album that contains songs for use with telling time.

## Art Experiences and Related Games, Crafts, and Projects

### 1. CREATING SYMMETRY*

MATERIALS: Drawing paper, crayons, paints, paste.

PROCEDURE: Present the following problem to the children. Picasso, the artist, is having six friends for lunch. He plans to serve pizza and wants each person to have one piece. He wants each piece of pizza to have exactly the same things on it as every other piece. In addition, he wants each piece to look the same as every other piece. What he wants is a completely symmetrical pizza. Can you design it? (See figure 6–18.)

This activity can be adapted for more mature students by simply requiring that each piece of pizza contain the same things. There are many other ways the pizza can be made symmetrical. In addition, odd numbers of pieces can be required for children who will be able to divide the circle properly.

*Contributed by Beverly Harrison, East Greenwich, R.I.

**Figure 6-18**

## 2. Creating Symmetry*

Materials: Drawing paper, scissors, white paper.

Procedure: Have the children write their names, in cursive writing, on a folded piece of drawing paper. Then instruct them to cut around the outside shape of the signature, open the paper, and paste it on a sheet of paper. From the results, they are to create a symmetrical picture. The completed drawings are shared and discussed. The children should note which inclusions are not symmetrical and how drawings could be improved to achieve symmetry. (See figure 6–19.)

*Contributed by Maureen Harrington, Westerly, R.I.

**1. Write**

Maureen

**2. Cut**

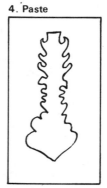

**3. Open**

**4. Paste**

**5. Create**

**Figure 6-19**

## 3. RECOGNIZING DIRECTION

MATERIALS: Drawing paper.
PROCEDURE: Have the children draw an intersection of two streets.

Start the activity by showing them where north, south, east, and west are on their drawings, and have them write in the directions. (See figure 6–20.) Then have the children draw according to instructions: "Put a traffic light on the north end of the street," "Draw a house on the northwest corner, a school building on the southwest corner," and so forth. More intersections can be added and the directions can become more complex, such as north-northeast.

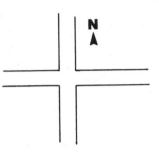

**Figure 6-20**

## 4. LOCATING DIRECTION

MATERIALS: Blank street maps of a town.

PROCEDURE: Have the children draw in the various things found in a town: city hall, library, fire department, police department, airport, and so forth, based on written instructions that are given on where to place the items according to cardinal directions. Compare and contrast the results.

## 5. GRAPHING

MATERIALS: Compass.

PROCEDURE: Have the children construct a circle graph and divide it into twenty-four hours. Then ask them to section off the graph to indicate the number of hours spent each day in particular activities, such as eating, sleeping, and playing.

## 6. GRAPHING

MATERIALS: Nothing special required.

PROCEDURE: The students are asked to conduct research on the use of some given product. Or, the students divide into groups and determine what product will be researched and how it will be researched. Students have chosen such topics as the kind of breakfast cereals eaten, the brands of toothpaste used, and favorite candy bars. Graphs are constructed to represent the research findings.

### 7. Finding Shapes

Materials: Road maps, tracing paper.
Procedure: Cover an area of a road map with tracing paper. The children must look for shapes created by the roads on the map and trace them (Wankelman et al., 1968, p. 66).

### 8. Finding Shapes

Materials: Drawing paper, crayons, paints, camera, film.
Procedure: Have the children identify geometric shapes in nature. They then draw or photograph them. The pictures are shared and the other children attempt to locate the shapes portrayed.

### 9. Using Measurement in Metrics

Materials: Drawing paper, tape measures, metric measures.
Procedure: Have the students draw an entire figure or a specific

Children of all ages can draw using shapes and symmetry. *(Reprinted by permission of the Montessori School, Iowa City, Iowa. Photograph by Rex Honey.)*

part of the body in proportion to the size of a human being. At first the students can experiment on themselves to determine the size of the head in relation to the rest of the body, the length of the arms and legs, and so forth. Their measurements should be converted to metric measurements and the drawings should be made using metrics.

## 10. Reference

*Pictorial Representation.* New York: John Wiley and Sons, 1967. This booklet presents many ideas for using pictures and graphs for communicating information.

# Drama Experiences and Related Games, Crafts, and Projects

## 1. Creating Symmetry

Materials: Nothing special required.
Procedure: Have the children create, through movement, a symmetrical shape with their bodies and then change the shape to an asymmetrical one. They can work alone, in twos, or in groups.

## 2. Locating Direction

Materials: Nothing special required.
Procedure: After teaching the directions of north, south, east, and west, divide the children into four groups. The children march to music in the direction of their group (north, east, south, or west). At a given time, the teacher calls out a direction and all the children turn and march in the direction called. To simplify things initially, it is best to have all the children moving in the same direction each time. To make the game more difficult, each group of children can be given a different direction in which to move.

## 3. Recognizing Direction

Materials: Nothing special required.
Procedure: One or two children are given a direction to act out with movement. The other children must try to guess which direction is being acted out. The children should be encouraged to be creative. They should go beyond cold for north and hot for south.

### 4. Making Shapes

MATERIALS:  A bolt of soft elastic tape, thread, needle.

PROCEDURE:  From a bolt of elastic tape, cut different lengths ranging in size from 1½ yards to 3 yards long. Sew the ends of each length together. Give a piece of tape to each child and instruct each one to make a different shape using the elastic. The child has to figure out how to do it. Examples of how to make a line, a triangle, and a square are shown in figure 6–21.

In addition to working alone, the children can work in groups and experiment making a circle, a star, and so forth. Figure 6–22 shows how a group can make a circle using ten children (Nash et al., 1977, p. 63).

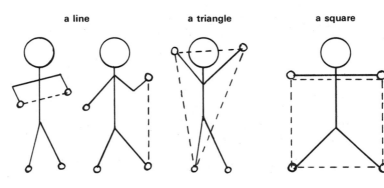

a line          a triangle          a square

**Figure 6-21**

**Figure 6-22**

### 5. Making Shapes

MATERIALS:  Nothing special required.

PROCEDURE:  Using movement, have the children see how many shapes they can make out of their own bodies without using any props. Then have the children join in groups of two or three or more to form as many shapes as possible out of their bodies. The rest of the children observe and try to determine the shape being made.

## 6. UNDERSTANDING THE CLOCK

MATERIALS: Number cards from 1 to 12, rhythm stick, hand drum.

PROCEDURE: Make a clock with twelve children. Each of the children should wear a number card from 1 to 12. To show that each number represents five minutes, place one child inside the circle, with a rhythm stick, and one child outside the circle, with a hand drum. Both children begin at number 12. The outside child walks five steps with five drumbeats to reach the child wearing number 1. The inside child also walks to number 1 but plays the rhythm stick only on the fifth beat. The children in the circle count to 5 with the drummer and clap on the fifth beat with the rhythm stick. The children should take turns being inside the circle, outside the circle, and a part of the circle (Nash et al., 1977, p. 56).

# REFERENCES

CROFT, DOREEN J., AND HESS, ROBERT D. *An Activities Handbook for Teachers of Young Children.* Boston: Houghton Mifflin Co., 1972.

JANIAK, WILLIAM. *Developing Everyday Skills* and *Songs About Me.* Long Branch, N.J.: Kimbo Educational. Records.

KAPLAN, SANDRA NINA; KAPLAN, JO ANN BUTOM; MADSEN, SHEILA KUMISHIMA; AND TAYLOR, BETTE K. *Change for Children.* Santa Monica: Goodyear Publishing Co., 1973.

KING, NANCY. *Giving Form to Feeling.* New York: Drama Book Specialists/Publishers, 1975.

KRANZ, STEWART, AND DELEY, JOSEPH. *The Fourth "R": Art for the Urban School.* New York: Van Nostrand Reinhold Co., 1970.

NASH, GRACE C.; JONES, GERALDINE W.; POTTER, BARBARA A.; AND SMITH, PATSY F. *The Child's Way of Learning.* Sherman Oaks, Calif.: Alfred Publishing Co., 1977.

PALMER, HAP. *Learning Basic Skills Through Music.* New York: Educational Activities. Records.

REICHARD, CARY L., AND BLACKBURN, DENNIS B. *Music Based Instruction for the Exceptional Child.* Denver: Love Publishing Co., 1973.

WANKELMAN, WILLARD F., WIGG, PHILLIP, AND WIGG, MARIETTA. *A Handbook of Arts and Crafts.* Dubuque, Iowa: William C. Brown Co., 1968.

WECHEMEYER, AVARIL, AND CEJKA, JOYCE. *Color by Number.* Denver: Love Publishing Co., 1979. Spirit masters.

# CHAPTER 7

# *Social Studies Experiences*

THE EXPERIENCES IN THIS CHAPTER are presented in the three broad skill areas that are the basic concerns of the social studies program: humanistic skills, intellectual skills, and social skills. In some instances, it is difficult to differentiate clearly exactly where an activity should be placed, since the experience may involve more than one goal. In each case, therefore, the activity has been placed according to its major emphasis.

## HUMANISTIC SKILLS

These skills involve ideals, values, attitudes, and beliefs. They deal mainly with other people and other cultures.

### Music Experiences and Related Games, Crafts, and Projects

1. UNDERSTANDING THE CULTURE

MATERIALS: Nothing special required.
PROCEDURE: Have the children research the songs and dances for a period, an event, or a person involved with music. When the research is completed, it is shared with the group and the reports are compared and

contrasted. Inferences are drawn about the period, country, or event from what is learned about the music of the times.

## 2. Understanding the Culture

Materials: Nothing special required.
Procedure: Have the children compare the works of specific musicians or composers from the same period and place and note the similarities and differences. The children share their research reports and compare and contrast their findings.

## 3. Relating Music to the Culture

Materials: Nothing special required.
Procedure: Assign specific composers to different children. Ask them to listen to recordings of the composer's works and to study the history of the period in which the composer lived. They are then to try to note how the work of the particular composer reflects his or her times. The children must substantiate their conclusions. The children share their reports and compare and contrast the inferences they have made.

## 4. Comparing Cultures

Materials: A variety of recorded music from various countries.
Procedure: Play a number of selections representing two or more countries. The children are to note the similarities and differences among the various styles of music. In addition to comparing extremes, such as Latin and Austrian music, it is interesting to compare the styles of music from a number of closely related countries, such as the various styles of African music.

## 5. Relating Music to the Culture

Materials: Ballads, folksongs, spirituals.
Procedure: Play a number of ballads, folksongs, or spirituals of a given time or place and have the children compare the contents and relate them to the particular time or place. Reference materials that can assist in the selection of these songs are listed at the end of this section.

## 6. Comparing Cultures

Materials: Recorded American and European blues.
Procedure: Teach the children about blues music. The European

blues has two or four lines in each stanza; the American blues has three lines. In addition, the first two lines of American blues are identical. Let the children listen to both American and European blues and discuss the differences they hear. When they have become familiar with blues, have them write their own blues songs to illustrate a particular historical event or to tell about a specific historical figure. They should be given opportunities to write both American and European blues songs.

## 7. COMPARING CULTURES*

MATERIALS: Piano, recorded Japanese music, pictures, and objects, tape recorder.

PROCEDURE: Introduce the children to music whose sounds are quite different from what they are accustomed to hear. Play some Japanese music softly in the background while displaying pictures and objects related to Japan. Then ask the children to listen to the music carefully and compare it with American music. What makes it sound different? Allow the children to go to the piano to discover which notes sound more Oriental. When they have all had a chance, introduce the pentatonic scale. Explain that the notes in the pentatonic scale are those heard when the five black keys in each octave on the piano are struck. Tell them that Japanese music as well as Indian and African chants are written using only the tones made by the black keys. Let each child create a Japanese song. No musical knowledge is necessary. Record the songs the children compose and then play back the tapes. The children may wish to create a dance to accompany their music. Or they may be taught the ribbon dance: they move to the music, twirling or moving streamers of crepe paper. The children can write lyrics about Japan to their Japanese melodies.

*Contributed by Maureen Harrington, Westerly, R. I.

## 8. UNDERSTANDING A CULTURE THROUGH DANCE*

MATERIALS: Nothing special required.

PROCEDURE: Have the children research the kinds of dances done by two different native American tribes, such as the Pueblo and the Plains Indians. Then list the names of the dances.

| PUEBLO | PLAINS |
|---|---|
| Sun Dance | Grass Dance |
| Rain Dance | Buffalo Dance |
| Harvest Dance | Scalp Dance |
| Snake Dance | War Dance |

Encourage the children to make inferences about the way each group of Indians lived. Let them learn some dances from each group and demonstrate them to the rest of the class.

*Contributed by Barbara Stock, North Kingstown, R. I.

## 9. Appreciating Music*

MATERIALS:  A variety of older and more recent recorded pop songs.

PROCEDURE:  Begin by playing one "oldie" and one recent pop-chart song with differences in tempo, texture, style, lyric, arrangement, and instrumentation. For example:

| | |
|---|---|
| Beatles (1960s) | BeeGees (1970s) |
| Elvis Presley (1950s) | Elton John (1970s) |
| Styx (1970s) | Rolling Stones (1960s) |

or

Beatles (early, 1960–1964; middle, 1965–1968; late, 1969–1971)
BeeGees (early, 1962–1964; middle, 1965–1976; late, 1977–present)

The objective is to gain an appreciation for music as representative of the culture from which it came. After the songs are played, compare the similarities and contrast the differences, musically and culturally/socially. In the 1950s the emphasis was on love and beaches; in the 1960s it was on protest; in the 1970s it was on disco.

Raise the question of whether music reflects the times or the times are influenced by music. A good example of the latter is the long hair style that became popular after the Beatles appeared.

Play classical pieces of music that illustrate differences. For example:

| | |
|---|---|
| Bach | Chopin |
| Liszt | Prokofiev |
| Mozart | (late) Beethoven |

or

Beethoven, early—middle—late

Compare similarities and differences musically and culturally. For example:

| | |
|---|---|
| Seventeenth century | Baroque |
| Eighteenth century | Rococo and Neo-Classical |
| Nineteenth century | Romantic (Impressionistic, and so forth) |

An extension, which overlaps with art, is to have the children find pictures of furniture, furnishings, and architecture, that correspond to music of the same vintage. Then compare the characteristics and find terms universal to these arts, such as "balance" and "elaborate."

Another extension would be to have the children study the lives of such furniture makers as Meeks, Belter, Chippendale, and Hepplewhite or such composers as Gottschalk, Mendelssohn, Bizet, and Rachmaninoff. Have the students note their similarities and differences, especially among artists of the same era.

*Contributed by Roberta M. Humble, Associate Professor of English, Rhode Island Junior College.

## 10. LEARNING ABOUT CULTURES

MATERIALS: A variety of folk dances on records or tapes as indicated in the individual descriptions that follow.

PROCEDURE: Teach the children folk dances of many different countries. This is an enjoyable experience for the children as well as an excellent learning experience. The folk dances and songs can enhance the learning of a particular historic period and, in addition, the children can be moved easily into more sophisticated music if it is so desired. After "Londonderry Air" the children could be exposed to Bach's "Air for the G String"; after an Hungarian folksong they might listen to Bartok's "Music for Children"; following a Russian folk dance, the music of Stravinsky could be introduced; and so forth.

Many folksongs and dances can be used in the classroom. Those described below represent a variety of countries around the world. They have been drawn from dances described by Fabricius (1971, chapter 7). Many variations in the movements and steps of each dance are possible. A number of sources for folksongs and dances are included in the reference section following the descriptions of the dances.

### American Folk Dances

*a. "Did You Ever See a Lassie?"*

MATERIALS: "Did You Ever See a Lassie?" (Bowmar #1511, RCA Victor #45-5066, Folkraft #1183).

PROCEDURE: Teach the words,

> Did you ever see a lassie, a lassie, a lassie,
> [or laddie if a boy is in the center]
> Did you ever see a lassie go this way and that?
> Go this way and that way, go this way and that way.
> Did you ever see a lassie go this way and that?

The children form a circle with one child selected as the central player. The children sing the first two lines and the circle moves to the right, walking in rhythm to the words. On the words "this way and that" the center player performs some movement or exercise. During the last two lines, the rest of the children imitate the leader's movement while singing. A new leader is chosen and the pattern is repeated. The movements must conform to the beat of the music.

### b. "Yankee Doodle"

MATERIALS: "Yankee Doodle" (Educational Activities, *Square Dancing*, #HYP1; Bowmar #1522; RCA Victor #45-5064).

PROCEDURE: A circle is formed with all the children facing counterclockwise.

Yankee Doodle went to town, riding on a pony.
[All the children skip or gallop eight steps forward.]
He stuck a feather in his cap and called it Macaroni.
[They all stop, face toward the center of the circle, pretend to put a feather in their caps, and bow on the word "Macaroni."]
Yankee Doodle, ha, ha, ha, Yankee Doodle dandy,
[The children join hands and take six slides to the right and stamp twice on the word "dandy."]
Yankee Doodle, ha, ha, ha, buy the girls some candy.
[The children slide six times to the left and clap their hands twice on the word, "candy."]

### c. "Paw Paw Patch"

MATERIALS: "Paw Paw Patch" (Educational Activities, #10, RCA Victor #45-5066).

PROCEDURE: The boys and girls stand in two parallel lines with the girls to the right of the boys. All face toward the head couple.

Where oh where is dear little . . .?
Where oh where is dear little . . .?
Where oh where is dear little . . .?
Way down yonder in the Paw Paw Patch.
[The head girl skips around the set, starting to her right. All the others stand and sing and clap. The first name of the head girl is used.]
Come on boys, let's go find her,
Come on boys, let's go find her,
Come on boys, let's go find her,
Way down yonder in the Paw Paw Patch.
[The head girl skips around the set again, followed by all the boys, until they are back in their original places.]
Picking up paw paws, put 'em in a basket,
Picking up paw paws, put 'em in a basket,
Picking up paw paws, put 'em in a basket,
Way down yonder in the Paw Paw Patch.

The head girl turns to her right, the head boy turns to his left. They skip to the end of the set followed by all the others. The head couple meet at the end of the set and form an arch with their joined hands. The rest of the couples go under the arch. The head couple is now the end couple. The couple who was the second couple is now the first. The game repeats with the new head couple. The dance continues until all the couples have had a chance to be head couple.

### d. "Pop Goes the Weasel"

MATERIALS: "Pop Goes the Weasel" (Educational Activities #AR46, RCA Victor #45-5066 and #45-6180).

PROCEDURE: The words of this song are well known. The children are divided into groups of three in which each child receives a number: 1, 2, or 3. Each group joins hands to form a small circle. The trios stand so that the small circles form one large circle. The groups of three skip to their left around their small circles for twelve skips. On the words "Pop goes the weasel," the number 1 child in each group is popped under the arms of the other two and moves up, counterclockwise, to the next group. The dance continues until all the children have had a chance to be "popped."

### e. "Oh Susanna"

MATERIALS: "Oh Susanna" (Educational Activities #HYP1, RCA Victor #45-6178).

PROCEDURE: The children form a single circle alternating boys and girls, with the girls to the right of their partners. All the children face the center of the circle.

Part I:  The girls take three steps to the center and quickly curtsy. Then they take three steps backward to place.

The boys take three steps to the center and quickly bow. Then they take three steps back to place.

All of Part I is repeated.

Part II:  The partners face each other. The girls will be facing clockwise and the boys will be facing counterclockwise. The right hand is extended to the partner, and the partners walk past each other passing right shoulders. The left hand is given to the next person, and these two people pass each other passing left shoulders. This continues until the children reach the seventh person, who becomes the new partner.

*Part III:* The boys put their new partners on their right. All join hands at shoulder height and walk around the circle until the music ends.

### f. "Patty Cake Polka"

MATERIALS: "Little Brown Jug" (Four Star #1365) or "Buffalo Gal" (Columbia #52007).

PROCEDURE: A double circle is formed with the boys on the inside facing the girls on the outside. Both hands are joined in each circle.

*Part I:* The boys put their left heels to the side and then their left toes behind the right feet. At the same time the girls put their right heels to the side and then their right toes behind their left feet. The procedure then is heel, toe; heel, toe; slide, two, three, four/heel, toe; heel, toe; slide, two, three, four. Then four slides counterclockwise (to the boys' left). The entire procedure is repeated using the opposite feet and moving in the opposite direction.

*Part II:* The children clap both hands together.

Next they clap partner's right hand with the right hand.

Then they clap their own hands together.

Next they clap partner's left hand with the left hand.

Then they clap their own hands together.

Next they clap both of partner's hands with both of theirs.

Then they clap their own hands together.

Finally, they clap their knees.

Next they hook right elbows with their partner and walk around eight counts taking eight steps. The boy moves ahead to the next partner and the dance is repeated.

### g. "Virginia Reel"

MATERIALS: "Virginia Reel" (Educational Activities #HYP4, RCA Victor #45-6180).

PROCEDURE: Four to six couples form two parallel lines with the girls' line to the right of the boys'. The lines face each other.

*Part I:* Each line walks three steps toward their partners, bows, walks three steps back, and pauses. This is repeated for sixteen counts (two sequences). Then the partners walk toward each other, grasp right hands, walk around each other, and walk back to place for sixteen counts. This is repeated with the left hand for sixteen counts. The procedure is repeated but with joining hands and walking first to the left and returning to place and then to the right and returning to place for sixteen counts. Once again the procedure is repeated with arms folded on the chest and passing first the left shoulders and returning to place and then the right shoulders and returning to place for another sixteen counts.

*Part II:*  The head couple comes to the center, joins hands, and slides eight slides down the center and eight slides back. Then they hook right elbows in the center and turn one and one-half times around until the girl faces the boys' line and the boy faces the girls' line. Each hooks left elbows with the next boy or girl and walks around that person and back to the partner. They hook elbows again and turn one and one-half times to face the next boy or girl, whose left elbows they hook and walk around. This procedure is continued with each person in the line until all have been "reeled." The original partners then join hands and slide up to the head of the set while the others stand and clap.

*Part III:*  The head girl turns to the right, the head boy turns to the left, and each child makes a U turn and follows the head of the line. At the foot of the set, the head couple forms an arch with their hands and all the couples pass through. The head couple is now the last couple and the second couple is now the first. The dance continues, repeating all the steps, with the new head couple. The dance is over when every couple has had a turn at being the head couple.


## Swedish Folk Dances

### a. "How D'Ye Do My Partner?"

MATERIALS:  "How D'Ye Do My Partner?" (Bowmar #1513, Folkraft #F1190).

PROCEDURE:  Form a double circle with the boys on the inside facing the girls on the outside.

> How d'ye do my partner? [boys bow]
> How d'ye do today? [girls curtsy]
> Will you dance in a circle? [partners shake right hands]
> I will show you the way. [partners shake left hands]

All the children skip counterclockwise holding their partner's inside hand. At the end of the chorus, the girl may move forward to the next boy and repeat the dance with the new partner.

### b. "I See You"

MATERIALS:  "I See You" (Bowmar #1518, Folkraft #1197).

PROCEDURE:  Form four parallel lines with everyone facing the center. The first line is a line of boys, then a line of girls, then another line of girls, and finally a line of boys.

| Boys | Girls | Girls | Boys |
|------|-------|-------|------|
| X | O | O | X |
| X | O | O | X |
| X | O | O | X |
| X | O | O | X |
| Face→ | | | ←Face |

I see you, I see you, tra la, tra la, tra la, tra la.
I see you, I see you, tra la, tra la, tra la, tra la.
[The boys put their hands on the shoulders of their girl partners and peek over the girls' shoulders at the opposite boy while bending from right to left in time with the music.]
You see me and I see you.
You take me and I take you.
[The boys skip to the center of the set, join hands with the opposite boy, and skip around to the left once.]

The last two lines of lyrics are repeated while the boys skip back to their partners, join hands, and skip around. Then, the places are exchanged so that the girls are behind the boys. The song is repeated with the girls performing the action.

### French Folk Dance: "Chimes of Dunkirk"

MATERIALS: "Chimes of Dunkirk" (Educational Activities #10, Folkraft #1188, RCA Victor #45-6176, Bowmar #1516).

PROCEDURE: A double circle is formed with the boys on the inside facing their partners, the girls, on the outside. Then, with arms stretched overhead and bending from side to side like a bell's pendulum: stamp, stamp, stamp/clap, clap, clap. Partners then join hands and run, or skip with small steps, in a small individual circle to the left returning to their original places. On the fourth and last phrase, the boys move up to the next girl. The procedure is then repeated. If the record has a chorus between verses, the pupils skip around the outside of the circle with their inside hands joined with their partner's.

### English Folk Dance: "A-Hunting We Will Go"

MATERIALS: "A-Hunting We Will Go" (Bowmar #1515, Folkraft #1191).

PROCEDURE: Four couples form two parallel lines with the boys in one line and the girls in the other. Everyone faces the center.

A hunting we will go,
A hunting we will go.
We'll catch a fox and put him in a box,
And then we'll let him go.

*Chorus*

A hunting we will go,
A hunting we will go.

On the first two lines, the head couple join hands in the center of the set and take seven slides down the center. On the last two lines, they slide seven slides back up to the head of the set.

*Chorus:*   The head couple drop hands. The boy skips to the left, the girl skips to her right, around the set. The couple meet at the foot of the set, join hands to form an arch, and the others follow the head couple and go through the arch. The dance is repeated with the new head couple.

## German Folk Dances

*a. "Children's Polka"*

MATERIALS: "Kinderpolka" (Bowmar #1519, RCA Victor #45-6179, Folkraft #1187).

PROCEDURE: The children form a circle alternating boy, girl, boy, girl. Partners face each other with the boys' left sides facing the center of the circle. The girls will have their right side facing the center. Partners join hands.

*Part I:*   Partners take two slides moving toward the center.

Partners stamp in place three times.

Partners take two slides moving back to place.

Partners stamp in place three times.

Repeat the above.

*Part II:*   The children clap their own thighs once.

The children clap their own hands once.

The children clap their partners' hands three times.

The last three steps are repeated.

The children shake their right fingers at their partners three times with the right elbow resting in the left hand.

The children shake their left fingers at their partners three times with their left elbows resting in their right hands.

Each child turns around in place, clapping hands over head or snapping fingers.

The rhythm is: slow, slow, fast, fast, fast.

*b. "Come Let Us Be Joyful"*

MATERIALS: "Come Let Us Be Joyful" (Educational Activities, *World of Fun,* record 7; RCA Victor #45-6177).

PROCEDURE: Lines of three are formed with a boy in the center holding the hands of a girl on each of his sides. Even numbers of trios are set up. Trio 1 faces trio 2, trio 3 faces trio 4, and so forth.

*Part I:*   Each line of three walks forward three steps toward the facing line, bows or curtsies, walks back three steps, and the children bring their feet together on the fourth count. This is repeated.

*Part II:*   The boy hooks right elbows with the girl on the right and skips around with her for four skips. The other girl skips in place. Then the boy hooks elbows with the girl on the left, skips around four skips with her, and the other girl skips in place.

*Part III:*   Part I is repeated by walking forward and backward three steps each way, walking forward eight steps, passing through the opposite trio, and going on to meet the next trio. The entire dance is then repeated with the new trio.

## Hungarian Folk Dance: "Cshebogar" (shay-bo-gar)

MATERIALS: "Cshebogar" (Educational Activities #10, RCA Victor #45-6182, Bowmar #1520).

PROCEDURE: A single circle is formed with everyone facing the center. Boys and girls are alternated, with the boy's partner to his left. Everyone joins hands.

*Part I:*   Take seven slides to the right, stopping on the count of eight.

Take seven slides to the left, stopping on the count of eight.

Take four skips toward the center and lean forward.

Take four skips back to place and raise the joined hands overhead.

Hook right arms with partners. Raise left arms above the head.

Take eight skips around with partner.

*Part II:*   Face partner with the boys' left sides toward the center of the circle. The boys place their hands on the girls' waists. The girls' hands are on the boys' shoulders. Each leans back, away from the other.

Partners take four slow slides toward the center and four slow slides back.

Partners take two slow slides toward the center and two slow slides back.

This is repeated, and the dance is ended with a shout.

## Danish Folk Dance: "Seven Jumps"

MATERIALS: "Seven Jumps" (Educational Activities, *World of Fun*, record 4; RCA Victor #45-6172).

PROCEDURE: A single circle is formed with all hands joined.

*Chorus:*   Seven slow skips to the right and one jump in place. Repeat going in the opposite direction.

*Step 1:*   Drop hands, put hands on hips. Raise right knee and hold until second note. Stand on third note. Repeat chorus.

*Step 2:*   Repeat step 1, add left knee. Repeat chorus.

*Step 3:*   Repeat steps one and two, add kneel on right knee. Repeat chorus.

*Step 4:*   Repeat the first three steps, add kneel on left knee. Repeat chorus.

*Step 5:*   Repeat the first four steps, add placing right elbow on the floor. Repeat chorus.

*Step 6:*   Repeat the first five steps, add placing left elbow on floor. Repeat chorus.

*Step 7:*   Repeat the first six steps, add placing forehead on the floor. Repeat chorus.

This dance may be done with only boys, only girls, or a mixed group.

## Mexican Folk Dance: "Chiapanecas"

MATERIALS: "Chiapanecas" (MacGregor #608).

PROCEDURE: Form a double circle with the boys on the inside and the girls on the outside. Partners face each other with both hands joined.

*Part I:*   Boys: Step left, swing right leg across left leg. Step right, swing left leg across right leg. Step left, swing right leg across left leg.

Girls do the same, starting with the right foot which, since they are facing the boys, is on the same side as the boys' left leg. They repeat the steps using the opposite leg each time.

*Part II:*   Balance, keeping hands joined. Step back, away from partner, step toward partner. Step back, away from partner. Clap twice. Step toward partner, step away from partner, step toward partner. Clap twice, the boy reaching around his partner's waist to clap and the girl clapping her hands behind her partner's head.

*Part III:*   Face counterclockwise, with inside hands joined, and move counterclockwise in time with the music.

Walk, walk, girl turns under boy's arm toward him.

Walk, walk, boy turns under girl's arm toward her.

Walk, walk, both turn toward each other.

Walk, walk, girl moves up to the next boy.

Clap twice.

## 11. REFERENCES

Association for Childhood Education International and Division of Christian Education, National Council of the Churches of Christ in the U.S.A. *Songs Children Like, Folk Songs from Many Lands.* Washington, D.C.: Association for Childhood Education International, 1958.

BAILEY, CHARITY, and HOLSAERT, EUNICE. *Sing a Song with Charity Bailey.* New York: Plymouth Music. Record.

BANNERMAN, GLENN. *Big Circle Mountain Square Dancing.* Freeport, N.Y.: Educational Activities, #AR52. Instructions are included.

BONI, MARGARET (ed.). *Fireside Book of Folk Songs.* New York: Simon and Schuster, 1947.

BRADFORD, LOUISE LARKINS. *Sing It Yourself.* Sherman Oaks, Calif.: Alfred Publishing Co., 1980. This book contains a comprehensive collection of 220 pentatonic American folk songs.

BRUMLEY, ALBERT E. *Songs of the Pioneers.* Camdenton, Mo.: Pioneer Song Book, 1970. This series of books contains a collection of songs and ballads.

DURLACHER, ED. *Square Dancing: Honor Your Partner.* Freeport, N.Y.: Educational Activities, #HYP 1, 2, 3, and 4. This series presents a progressive course in square dancing with talk-through instructions.

*Ethnic Dances of Black People Around the World.* Deal, N. J.: Kimbo Educational Records, #9040. Eight ethnic dances are taught with oral directions.

GLASS, HENRY BUZZ, and HALLUM, ROSEMARY. *Dances Around the World.* Freeport, N.Y.: Educational Activities, 1976, #AR572. Folk dances for upper elementary through adult are included. Ten different nations are represented, and directions are included for all the dances.

*Honor Your Partner.* Freeport, N.Y.: Educational Activities, 1975, #10. This album is intended for grades 2 through 4. Instructions are included on the record, and directions appear on the album. The dances include American, French, Hungarian, Danish, Mexican, and American Indian.

HOWARD, CAROLE. *Authentic Indian Dances and Folklore.* Deal, N.J.: Kimbo Educational Records, 1971, #9070. Four dances of the Chippewa tribe are included: the Corn Dance, Rain Dance, War Dance, and Strawberry Dance. Directions are on the record. Explanations and meanings of the dances are also included. The teachers manual contains full instructions for each dance along with illustrations and suggestions for dance variations. In addition, directions are included for rhythmic craft projects.

JERVEY, ARDEN, and PITTMAN, ANNE. *Beginners' American Folk Dances.* Deal, N.J.: Kimbo Educational Records, 1966, #LP3040. The album contains polkas, schottisches, stamping two-step, and fleet foot two-step dances. Directions are printed on the album cover. A manual is also included. Though this album contains American dances, many Russian, Yugoslavian, and German dances utilize the schottische and the polka also is a popular dance in many European countries.

LOMAX, JOHN A., and LOMAX, ALAN. *Folk Song, U.S.A.* New York: New American Library, 1975. This book contains 111 American ballads with descriptions and explanations of each song.

MONTEGO, JOE. *Authentic Afro-Rhythms.* Deal, N.J.: Kimbo Educational Records, #6060. Rhythms from six different countries are included.

*New World Record.* The Recorded Anthology of American Music, Dept. B, 3 East 54 Street, NY 10022. This anthology contains 100 records tracing, through music, the cultural and social history of the United States.

PALMER, HAP. *Simplified Folk Songs.* Freeport, N.Y.: Educational Activities, #AR518. These songs, aimed at the primary grades, are available on both record and cassette.

# Art Experiences and Related Games, Crafts, and Projects

### 1. UNDERSTANDING THE CULTURE

MATERIALS: Materials to make hats.

PROCEDURE: Have the children make hats representing a particular time and place. Some suggestions are military hats, ceremonial hats, men's dress hats, women's dress hats, and women's daytime hats. A variation is for the hats to represent development over time and be related to changes in the culture.

### 2. DEVELOPING UNDERSTANDING

MATERIALS: Construction paper, rolls of paper, newspaper, paste, crayons, paints.

PROCEDURE: Using paper, have children create costumes, settings, and environments for a particular event, era, or location. Rolled-up newspaper can be made into swords, pieces of paper can be snow, and paper can be shaped into costumes and props (King, 1975, p. 229).

### 3. REPRODUCING HISTORY

MATERIALS: Scrap materials, such as wood pieces, beads, foil, wool, ribbon, buttons, pine cones, seeds, twigs, and feathers; books and pictures on folk art.

PROCEDURE: Ask the children to look through the books and pictures and find some folk-art craft object they would like to try to make. Examples of items that can be made are whistles, banks, spinning toys, dolls, weather vanes, and store signs (Corwin, 1974, p. 12).

### 4. UNDERSTANDING POINTS OF VIEW

MATERIALS: Cartoon and print broadsides.

PROCEDURE: Let the children view cartoon and print broadsides about some of the following events as the Americans and the British might have viewed them: Boston Tea Party, effects of the Stamp Act, passage of the Quartering Act, signing of the Declaration of Independence. Have the students create their own cartoons and broadsides for historical and contemporary events (Corwin, 1974, p. 10).

### 5. DEVELOPING INSIGHT

MATERIALS: Pictures of such things as native American blankets, elk or buffalo paintings, and pictographs. If the real items are available, they are more effective.

PROCEDURE: Have the children examine the picture or item carefully. Then, through discussion, let the children determine how much they can tell about the native American tribal life from each of the crafts. They can then do some research to find out how accurate their determinations were.

## 6. DEVELOPING UNDERSTANDING

MATERIALS: Puppet materials, large paper, paints.

PROCEDURE: To better understand the culture and the people of a given time or place, have the children set up a puppet show. They should determine what characters they will portray, what event they will enact, and how they will enact it. They then create the scenery, the puppets, and the props. They write the script, bearing in mind how the characters would react. After putting on the show, they exchange roles in order to develop a better understanding of the different characters. Or, in place of writing a script, they may role play.

## 7. UNDERSTANDING THE CULTURE*

MATERIALS: Postage stamps.

PROCEDURE: Bring in and have the children bring in stamps, stamp collections, and reference books about stamps. Through study of the stamps, history can be revealed; for example, the role of women in American life can be studied by having the children determine how many American women have been honored on stamps, the roles women assume on stamps, and so forth. The stamps of any country can be used, as well as almost any theme. In addition, the stamps of various countries can be compared and contrasted in respect to a particular theme.

*Contributed by Kathy McGregor, Narragansett, R. I.

## 8. UNDERSTANDING THE CULTURE

MATERIALS: Works of a few artists from the same period and place.

PROCEDURE: Have the children compare the works of a few artists from the same time period and place to note similarities in respect to subject and theme. Lead them to see that the history of a period is reflected in its artwork.

## 9. COMPARING CULTURES

MATERIALS: Artworks made in different countries at different times.

PROCEDURE: Have the children note the similarities and differences of various styles of art from other countries and from different time periods. The various styles reflect the particular culture and the specific time period.

## 10. DEVELOPING UNDERSTANDING

MATERIALS: Construction paper, paint, crayons, glue, string, yarn, and other items to decorate a mask.

PROCEDURE: Establish a specific country and time period. Have the children determine historical figures who lived during that time in that place. Then have each child create a three-dimensional mask for a different historical figure. When the masks are completed, have the children put them on and assume the identities of the individuals they represent. Present a specific incident, real or fictional, and have the children describe how their character would act and feel in the situation. The presentations should be true to the period and to the individuals portrayed. The group then discusses the presentations' authenticity.

## 11. UNDERSTANDING HOLIDAYS*

MATERIALS: Art paper, crayons, paints, poster board.

PROCEDURE: Have the children research important holidays in different selected countries. Then have them discuss each holiday in respect to the dates, the importance of the celebration, important people involved, etc. Working in small groups, children cut a piece of poster board into the shape of the country whose holiday the group will be depicting in the form of a mural. Accuracy in detail should be stressed. Suggested holidays include: U.S., Fourth of July; Mexico, Cinco de Mayo; Ireland, St. Patrick's Day; Israel, Feast of Purim; China, New Year's Day; France, Bastille Day. The purpose of this activity is to make the children aware of the importance of special holidays in other countries and to compare and contrast these with those celebrated in the U.S. The children could also compare the different ways the same holiday is celebrated in various countries. For example, Christmas and Independence Day celebrations in various countries could be compared.

*Contributed by Patty Dickens, Reno, Nevada.

## 12. REFERENCES

GLUBOK, SHIRLEY. This author has written twenty-five books, each devoted to the art of a different country or era. Some of the books are on architecture. They are available through Macmillan, Harper, and Atheneum book companies.

GRISWOLD, VERA JO, and STARKE, JUDITH. *Multi-Cultural Art Projects*. Denver: Love Publishing Co., 1980. Projects for twenty-seven different countries, from Africa to the Ukraine, are presented.

HODGES, WALTER. *Shakespeare's Theater*. London: Coward Book Co., 1964.

KINNEY, JEAN, and KINNEY, CLE. *21 Kinds of American Folk Art and How to Make Each One*. New York: Atheneum, 1972. This book includes a description of each folk art, who practiced it, when and where it developed, and how to create it.

LEACROFT, HELEN, and LEACROFT, RICHARD. *The Buildings of Ancient Man*. Menlo Park, Calif.: Addison-Wesley, 1973.

MACAULAY, DAVID. *Cathedral: The Story of Its Construction*. Boston: Houghton Mifflin, 1973.

*Meet the Artist Series*. New York: Random House. Each filmstrip in this series relates the artist to his or her times or to a historical event depicted by the artist.

## Drama Experiences and Related Games, Crafts, and Projects

### 1. UNDERSTANDING OTHER CULTURES

MATERIALS: Construction paper, cardboard, paints, decorating materials.

PROCEDURE: Have the children make copies of African or native American masks. When they are completed, the children role play a historical event or custom.

### 2. UNDERSTANDING ATTITUDES AND BELIEFS

MATERIALS: Nothing special required.

PROCEDURE: Assign each child a different historical figure to role play. The figures selected should be from different eras and locales. Then assign a topic, such as capital punishment or war. The characters come together, out of history, to discuss the topic from their own vantage points. The discussions must be accurate to the characters and the times. The remaining children listen to the discussion and then make comments and criticisms about the reality of the portrayals. All criticisms must be supported by evidence.

## INTELLECTUAL SKILLS

The intellectual skills involve acquiring knowledge to achieve goals. They involve learning facts about eras, events, places, and people as well as map work.

## Music Experiences and Related Games, Crafts, and Projects

### 1. Reporting Through Music

Materials: Nothing special required.

Procedure: Select a historical period, event, or individual. Break the students into groups and have each group prepare a report for the others. Each report must be related to music. One group may learn a dance of the period, another folksongs about an event, another the composers of the period, and so forth.

### 2. Composing Historical Songs

Materials: Nothing special required.

Procedure: After the children have learned about ballads and have listened to a few, have them write a ballad to depict a specific event in history. The contents of the ballad must be accurate. The children sing their songs to the others. The songs are then discussed in respect to major items omitted or inaccuracies. As an example, using the melody of "Yankee Doodle," a student started a ballad, on the theme of "A Highlight of 1980," this way:

> 1980 was the year
> A president elected.
> We all went out to cast a vote,
> and Reagan was selected.

The students may wish to present their ballads for an assembly program or to another class.

### 3. Learning Facts

Materials: Nothing special required.

Procedure: Have the students do some research to locate songs about a place being studied or songs composed during a particular time being studied. Compare and contrast these pieces of music in respect to the accuracy of the facts contained in the lyrics.

### 4. Relating History in Song

Materials: Nothing special required.

Procedure: Provide an event or an individual. Then give the children the first line for a song to tell about the event or individual. Each child in the group must then contribute an additional line until the song is finished. The words can be written on the board as the children contribute them. Make up a melody or use a simple melody with which the children are all familiar. Discuss important details that have been omitted, any inaccuracies in the song, and so forth.

## 5. LEARNING FACTS*

MATERIALS: Songs about sheep.

PROCEDURE: Present a few songs about sheep, such as "Baa, Baa, Black Sheep" or "Sheep Shearing" (Silver Burdett Co., *Making Music Your Own,* grade 2). Teach the songs and then discuss what sweaters are made of, where wool comes from, how wool is made into yarn. The children then research how cloth is made today and how it was woven many years ago. Those students who know how to knit can demonstrate for the others. A knitting lesson might follow.

*Contributed by Kathy McGregor, Narragansett, R. I.

## 6. REFERENCES

GALLINA, JILL. *Holiday Songs for All Occasions.* Long Branch, N.J.: Kimbo Educational, #KIM0805.

*Making Music Your Own.* Morristown, N.J.: Silver Burdett Co., 1971.

PALMER, HAP. *Holiday Songs and Rhythms.* Freeport, N.Y.: Educational Activities, #AR538.

# Art Experiences and Related Games, Crafts, and Projects

## 1. LEARNING FACTS

MATERIALS: Artwork of a particular period.

PROCEDURE: Have the children research the artwork of a particular period. They must compare and contrast the works in respect to the facts presented in them.

## 2. ANALYZING CRITICALLY

MATERIALS: Nothing special required.

PROCEDURE: A research project is set up. The children must find a series of artworks that depict the same historical event, even if from different aspects. *America in Art, The American Revolution* (Corwin, 1974), for example, documents America's struggle for freedom using approximately 130 paintings.

The students present the events through the series of artworks. A discussion of the presentation follows each report.

The students should be led to discover how their views of history are affected by the works of art. If an event involved two different countries, it is most interesting for the students to compare and contrast works by artists of these countries.

The students should also learn something about the artists themselves. Were they alive during the time they depicted, or were their paintings based on some recorded event about which they read? How might these situations affect the validity of the piece of art?

### 3. LEARNING FACTS

MATERIALS: Pictures of buildings from various periods.
PROCEDURE: Have the children examine the architecture of various periods and compare and contrast periods and/or countries in respect to the materials used, the style, and so forth.

### 4. NOTING CHANGE

MATERIALS: Pictures of fashions from various periods.
PROCEDURE: Have the children compare the fashions of various periods within a country or various countries within the same time period. Discuss the reasons for the different clothing styles, for changes in style, and so forth. The children may make an illustrated time line of changes in fashion for men and women of a particular country.

### 5. MOTIVATING THOUGHT

MATERIALS: A drawing or painting.
PROCEDURE: Use a picture to initiate a unit of study. Show a picture of an Indian village and raise such questions as: What are the Indians wearing? What might the clothes be made of? What animals would have to be available? What are the homes made of? What materials would have to be available? From where might these materials come? The children speculate about answers to the questions. During the study unit that follows, the children attempt to determine the answers to the questions raised and see if their original thinking was correct.

### 6. RECOGNIZING KEY EVENTS

MATERIALS: Cardboard or oak tag, pencil, white glue, string, foil, black spray paint, paper towels.

PROCEDURE: Have the children make coins for a particular country during a specific time period or for a continuing period of time. The decision making that goes into the selection of what to put on the coins is important. The children must select only noteworthy things.

To make the coins:

a. Draw a circle on cardboard or oak tag.
b. In the circle, with pencil, draw the picture decided upon.
c. Put lines of white glue over the pencil lines and press string into the glue.
d. When dry, cover the coin with foil and smooth the foil so that the lines of the string show through.
e. Spray the coin with black paint. Wait five seconds and wipe the paint off with paper toweling (Longo, 1975, unnumbered card).

## 7. REPRODUCING HISTORY

MATERIALS: Drawing paper, crayons, paints.

PROCEDURE: Have the children create a group picture of a country, a place, or an event by having small groups of two or three children assume responsibility for different aspects of the environment, for example, the wildlife, the street scene, the dress of the people. Some research or discussion is needed initially. The amount and kind will depend upon the ability of the children to determine the information themselves. The children should meet and discuss the organization of the group painting and the function of each of the smaller groups. This activity is also good for developing social skills.

## 8. RECOGNIZING KEY EVENTS

MATERIALS: Drawing paper, crayons, paints.

PROCEDURE: Have the children design a flag for a state, a country, or a continent. The flag should represent historically significant events. The children should justify the inclusion of specific things in their flags. This activity presents a good opportunity for teaching the children about symbolic representation.

## 9. RESEARCHING FACTS

MATERIALS: Fabric, thread, needles, scissors.

PROCEDURE: Have the children research the uniforms worn by the military personnel of a country during a specific time period. A great deal can be learned about the country or the period from this project. In addition to researching the uniforms, the children can attempt to make the different kinds of uniforms, being as accurate as possible in representation. The children can research the fabrics used and the names of the various parts of the uniform and items the military men carried. In the picture shown here, for example, the boy is a member of the Second Rhode Island Regiment of the Continental Line. He made his musician's uniform himself, and every part of it is authentic. The coat is made of bleached linen, the overalls are bleached Irish linen, the shirt is muslin, and the shoes are leather. The drum has a calfskin head and catgut snare. The rope is linen. His haversack holds authentic reproductions of the money of the time; his blanket is of 16-ounce white wool.

A musician's uniform from the Second Rhode Island Regiment of the Continental Line. *(Reprinted with the permission of Claudette Donnelly. Photograph by Lewis S. List.)*

## 10. Noting Change

Materials: Drawing paper, crayons, paints.

Procedure: Select something that has changed over the years. Have the children draw pictures to represent the change. Changes in the electric light, in the telephone, and so forth, are typical examples. Forte et al. (1973) suggest that the contrast can be done for either the past, present, or the future. A child can pretend to be in the year 2050 and invent a new means of transportation. The child draws it and then tells the way it moves, the materials it is made of, and the tools needed to make it.

## 11. Applying Knowledge

Materials: Drawing paper, crayons.

Procedure: Tell the children to pretend that Paul Revere had to warn them of danger but did not know where they lived. Have them make an illustrated map of the route from school to their homes to show the way. They should include houses, churches, fences, and so forth (Longo, 1975, unnumbered card).

## 12. Integrating Skills

Materials: Cardboard or oak tag, state map, crayons.

Procedure: Make a "Spin the Miles" game (figure 7–1). Draw a picture of a car; make two of the wheels spinners. Using a map of any state, mark the names of various cities on each spinner. The child spins both spinners and then must determine the distance between the two cities using the map (Kaplan et al., 1973, p. 65). The children can be asked to draw the pictures and make their own "Spin the Miles" games. More than one state can be used so that the children are measuring distances between cities in two different states.

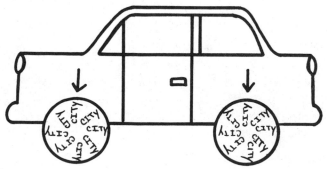

**Figure 7-1**

## 13. APPLYING KNOWLEDGE*

MATERIALS: Drawing paper, papier-mâché, paints, cardboard, wheat paste.

PROCEDURE: After teaching all the necessary topological terms, ask the children to map an imaginary island. All these terms must be included on their islands. Once the island is mapped, it is constructed out of papier-mâché, painted, and named.

First the children outline the shape of the island on cardboard or plywood. They make papier-mâché by passing newspaper strips through wheat paste and placing the strips on the island's outline. Then the areas where mountains and plateaus are desired are built up.

After the construction has dried for two days, the water is painted blue and the rest of the island is painted the colors desired. A key should be developed for the colors of the land areas.

After allowing the paint to dry overnight, the children label all parts. The children name their island and all the places on it. The names should all relate; for example, Treat Island could have a Peppermint Bay, a Chocolate City, and so forth.

There are many extensions for this project. The island could be designed for specific coordinates on a world map. The children would then have to describe the climate, the vegetation, and so forth. The children could also determine the distance of their islands to specific other places in the world.

Travel brochures, advertising the islands, could be designed. The brochures should include pictures and a written description. Or, a factual article for an encyclopedia could be written about the island. The article would have to include a map, a flag, island birds and animals, and so forth. Older children could be asked to write a constitution and laws for their islands.

*Contributed by Barbara Stock, North Kingstown, R. I.

## 14. RECREATING FASHION

MATERIALS: Fabric, thread, needles, staples.

PROCEDURE: Let the children make doll clothes and dress dolls to represent different countries and different periods in history.

## 15. RECREATING FACES

MATERIALS: Round tube containers, scissors, glue, yarn, construction paper, buttons.

PROCEDURE: After studying a particular period or event in history, have each child decide upon a particular historical figure as a secret model. Using the pictures and information in the history books, the children try to reproduce the expression, hair coloring, eyes, and so forth, of the secret model. The tube containers are used for the faces. The finished models are displayed on a table, and the rest of the group tries to guess who each face is supposed to represent. (Suggested by Taylor et al., 1979, task 93.)

## Drama Experiences and Related Games, Crafts, and Projects

### 1. LEARNING FACTS

MATERIALS: Movie camera, film.

PROCEDURE: Have the children write a script for a film depicting an event or the life of an individual. Parts are assigned and the children narrate or act out the situation.

### 2. LEARNING FACTS

MATERIALS: Puppet-making supplies.

PROCEDURE: Have the children make puppets of famous people and then act out the lives of the individuals. Groups of children can work together so that the people connected with the famous person will also be depicted in puppet form. Or, the children can act out a historical event in which the person was involved.

### 3. APPLYING KNOWLEDGE

MATERIALS: Oak tag, clay, sand, chicken wire, newspaper, wheat paste, masking tape, scraps of cloth, assorted papers, glue, paints.

PROCEDURE: Give the students a verbal description of a state. They are told the state's size and terrain. They then must interpret how the state should look in terms of the size of the mountains, the color of the soil, the shape of the state, and so forth. Each student discusses and draws an interpretation of the state. The class selects one picture to be used as a model and begins making a map. The state's cities, products, and people are researched as the map progresses. The students are able to learn about their subject and also to learn how to make relief sculptures (Carter and Adams, 1978, p. 58).

## SOCIAL SKILLS

The social skills are those that lead to good citizenship. They include learning about the community and about how to get along with others.

## Music Experiences and Related Games, Crafts, and Projects

### 1. DEVELOPING CITIZENSHIP

MATERIALS: Nothing special required.
PROCEDURE: Ask the children to make a list of things they feel are good and bad for people in a society to do. They should substantiate every item on the list in respect to its effects on society and take care not to pass judgment. The lists are compared and contrasted and discussed. Then the children are asked to make up songs about how people should and should not act if they are going to be good citizens. Older children can compare good acts of citizenship under different forms of government.

### 2. RECOGNIZING THE IMPORTANCE OF OTHERS

MATERIALS: Nothing special required.
PROCEDURE: After discussing the roles of various community helpers, have the children write their own song lyrics about these people, noting in particular the things they do to assist others and how they must feel. As with any activity in which children compose lyrics, it is best to work with well-known, simple melodies.

### 3. LEARNING ABOUT INTERDEPENDENCE

MATERIALS: Nothing special required.
PROCEDURE: Have the children determine and discuss as many musical situations as possible in which people must work together, for example, bands and orchestras, quartets, duets. Discuss what has to happen in order for a group to have a successful musical presentation. The children should be led to see the need to have a leader, to follow rules, and to work together cooperatively.

### 4. LEARNING TO COOPERATE

MATERIALS: Nothing special required.
PROCEDURE: Set up situations in which the children must work

together cooperatively. One child may write a melody and the other the lyrics; one child may play the music and the other may dance or sing. Discuss the problems that arose and how they were or could be resolved.

## Art Experiences and Related Games, Crafts, and Projects

### 1. UNDERSTANDING THE COMMUNITY*

MATERIALS: "The Good Old Days" special in a newspaper.

PROCEDURE: Show the children the "before" and "after" pictures in a local newspaper that runs a section on "then and now." Frequently there is a picture of a city block fifty years ago and that same street today.

Have the children work in small groups, each group using a different set of pictures, and discuss such things as what changes have been made, how the changes were made, how the changes affected the lives of the people, how the changes affected the environment, and what time period the children prefer and why.

*Contributed by Maureen Harrington, Westerly, R. I.

### 2. LEARNING TO COOPERATE

MATERIALS: Art paper, paints.

PROCEDURE: Set up situations in which the children must work cooperatively in an art project. Each child may be responsible for a different aspect of the project. When the activity is completed, have the children discuss the importance of the role of each child in the total project, the problems that arose, and the ways the problems were or could have been resolved.

### 3. DEVELOPING CITIZENSHIP SKILLS

MATERIALS: Drawing paper, crayons, paints.

PROCEDURE: Have the children make posters advertising good citizenship qualities. Each poster could concern itself with a different aspect of citizenship. A class mural could then be made using the individual posters.

### 4. LEARNING ABOUT THE COMMUNITY*

MATERIALS: Clay, poster board.

PROCEDURE: After studying the many components of a community, the students are given modeling clay and asked to make something that would be a necessary part of a community. When they have finished, a piece of poster board is placed on the floor to represent the land upon which the community will be built. The children share their clay pieces with the others, explain the function each piece serves, why it is important to the community, and place the item somewhere in the community explaining why that particular location is good for that item.

When all the items have been placed, a discussion is held on the final product. Topics include: Is anything missing? Are the locations convenient for the welfare of the entire community?

The finished product is painted and decorated.

*Contributed by Azy Marini, Sparks, Nevada.

### 5. REFERENCE

CARMICHAEL, VIOLA S. 1971. Many possible art activities for such topics as homes, families, occupations, and transportation are presented.

## Drama Experiences and Related Games, Crafts, and Projects

### 1. LEARNING TO COOPERATE

MATERIALS: Nothing special required.
PROCEDURE: Select a real animal, such as an elephant. Using a group of five or six students, create the animal. Appropriate sounds and movements should be included. Set up an imagined area for the animal to move through, or have two animals meet and interact. Then discuss the way it feels to be one part of the total, the advantages of working as a group, and the disadvantages (King, 1975, pp. 122, 123).

### 2. LEARNING ABOUT INTERDEPENDENCE

MATERIALS: Nothing special required.
PROCEDURE: Set up certain movement activities that would be very difficult, if not impossible, for one child to do alone. Then assign an individual child to try to work out the movement. Lead the children to see that more than one person is needed to do the movement. Get them into a discussion of how and when people need each other in order to live. Talk about such items as food supplies and housing.

# REFERENCES

CARMICHAEL, VIOLA S. *Curriculum Ideas for Young Children.* Los Angeles: Southern California Association for the Education of Young Children, 1971.

CARTER, C. DOUGLAS, and ADAMS, JAMES A. "ABC Program." *Music Educator's Journal* (January 1978): 56–58.

CORWIN, SYLVIA K. *America in Art, The American Revolution.* Teacher's Manual. New York: Miller-Brody Productions, 1974.

FABRICIUS, HELEN. *Physical Education for the Classroom Teacher.* Dubuque, Iowa: William C. Brown, 1971.

FORTE, IMOGENE, PRANGLE, M. and TUPA, ROBBIE. *Center Stuff For Nooks, Crannies, and Corners.* Nashville: Incentive Publications, 1973.

KAPLAN, SANDRA NINA; KAPLAN, JO ANN BUTOM; MADSEN, SHEILA KUNISHIMA; and TAYLOR, BETTE K. *Change for Children.* Santa Monica: Goodyear Publishing Co., 1973.

KING, NANCY. *Giving Form to Feeling.* New York: Drama Book Specialists/Publishers, 1975.

LONGO, VICKY. *Bicentennial Art Cards.* Washington, D.C.: The Center for Applied Research in Education, 1975.

TAYLOR, FRANK D., ARTUSO, ALFRED A., and HEWETT, FRANK M. *Creative Art Tasks for Children.* Denver: Love Publishing Co., 1970.

# Additional References

*Arts Impact: Curriculum for Change. A Summary Report*. University Park: The Pennsylvania State University Press, 1973.

BICCHIERE, ROCCO. *Let's Sing a Yiddish Song*. New York: Kinderbuch Publications, 1970.

BLOOM, KATHRYN. "Strengthening and Expanding the Arts in School." *The National Elementary Principal* (January/February 1976): 37–44.

———. "The Arts in Education: A New Movement." In *Arts in Education Partners*, edited by N. Shuker. New York: The John D. Rockefeller III Fund, 1977.

BOORMAN, JOYCE. *Creative Dance in the First Three Grades*. New York: David McKay Co., 1969.

———. *Creative Dance in Grades Four to Six*. Don Mills, Ontario: Longman's of Canada, 1971.

BRANDER, MICHAEL. *Scottish and Border Battles and Ballads*. New York: Clarkson N. Potter, Inc., 1975.

BRITTEN, BENJAMIN, and HOLST, IMOGENE. *The Wonderful World of Music*. Garden City, N. Y.: Doubleday and Co., 1958.

CHASE, RICHARD. *American Folk Tales and Songs*. New York: Dover, 1971.

CROWINSHIELD, ETHEL. *Stories That Sing*. Boston: Boston Music Co., 1955.

DIETZ, BETTY WARNER, and PARK, THOMAS CHOONBAI. *Folk Songs of China, Japan, Korea*. New York: John Day, 1964.

FOWKE, EDITH. *Canadian Folk Songs*. Baltimore, Md.: Penguin, 1973.

GROETZINGER, ISABELLE, and GODE, MARGUERITE. *Play and Sing, Hayes Action Song Book for Kindergarten and Primary*. Wilkinsburg, Pa.: Hayes School Publishing Co., 1958.

HARDIMAN, GEORGE W., and ZERNICH, THEODORE. *Art Activities for Children.* Englewood Cliffs, N.J.: Prentice-Hall, 1981.

HEALY, JAMES N. *Irish Ballads and Songs of the Sea.* Cork, Ireland: The Mercier Press, 1971.

HILL, MARGOT HAMILTON, and BUCKNELL, PETER A. *Evolution of Fashion: Pattern and Cut from 1066 to 1930.* New York: Reinhold Publishing Corp., 1967.

HUNT, LESLIE L. *25 Kites that Fly.* New York: Dover Publications, 1971.

JENKINS, ELLA. *The Ella Jenkins Song Book.* New York: Oak Publications, 1971.

JOLLIFE, MAUREEN. *The Third Book of Irish Ballads.* Cork, Ireland: The Mercier Press, 1970.

JONES, BESSIE, and HAWES, BESS LOMAX. *Step It Down.* New York: Harper and Row, 1972.

JONES, LEROI. *Blues People.* New York: William Morrow and Co., 1970.

KARSTADT, ROBERTA. "Tracing and Writing Activities for Teaching Reading." *Reading Teacher* (December 1976): 297–98.

KEMP, DAVID. *A Different Drummer, An Ideas Book for Drama.* Toronto, Ontario: McClelland and Stewart Ltd., 1972.

LABAN, RUDOLF. *Modern Educational Dance.* London: MacDonald and Evans, Ltd., 1968.

LANDECK, BEATRICE. *Echoes of Africa in Folk Songs of the Americas.* New York: David McKay Co., 1961.

———. *Songs to Grow On.* New York: Edward B. Marks Music Corp.; William Sloane Associates, 1950.

———, and CROOK, ELIZABETH. *Wake Up and Sing!* New York: Edward B. Marks Music Corp.; William Morrow and Co., 1969.

LLOYD, A. L. *Folk Songs in England.* New York: International Publishers, 1970.

LOVELL, JOHN. *Black Song: The Forge and the Flame—The Story of How the Afro-American Spiritual was Hammered Out.* New York: MacMillan, 1972.

McCASLIN, NELLIE. *Children and Drama.* New York: David McKay Co., 1975.

———. *Creative Dramatics in the Classroom.* New York: David McKay Co., 1968.

McLAUGHLIN, ROBERTA, and SCHLIESTETT, PATTI. *The Joy of Music, Early Childhood.* Evanston, Ill.: Sunny-Birchand Co., 1967.

MAKEBA, MIRIAM. *The World of African Song.* Chicago, Ill.: Quadrangle Books, 1971.

MASON, BERNARD S. *Drums, Tomtoms and Rattles.* New York: Dover Publications, 1974.

MATHIAS, SANDRA, and FANYO, MARY. "Blending Reading Instruction with Music and Art." *Reading Teacher* (February 1977): 497–500.

MAY, FRANK B. *Teaching Language as Communication to Children.* Columbus, Ohio: Charles E. Merrill, 1967.

MORTON, ROBIN. *Folksongs Sung in Ulster.* Cork, Ireland: The Mercier Press, 1970.

*Music Educators Journal* (January 1978). Entire issue devoted to The Arts in Education.

PALMER, ROY, *A Touch on the Times*. Ontario, Canada: Penguin, 1974.

PAREDES, AMERICO. *A Texas-Mexican Cancionero—Folksongs of the Lower Border*. Urbana, Ill.: University of Illinois Press, 1976.

PAYNTER, JOHN, and ASTON, PETER. *Sound and Silence*. Cambridge, England: University Press, 1970.

PLATT, PENNY. "Grapho-Linguistics: Children's Drawings in Relation to Reading and Writing Skills." *Reading Teacher* (December 1977): 262–68.

RUSSELL, JOAN. *Creative Dance in the Primary School*. New York: Oak Publications, 1964.

RUSSELL, TONY. *Blacks, Whites and Blues*. New York: Stein and Day, 1970.

SAINTE-MARIE, BUFFY. *The Buffy Sainte-Marie Songbook*. New York: Grosset and Dunlap, 1971.

SCHAFER, WILLIAM J., and RIEDEL, JOHANNES. *The Art of Ragtime*. New York: Da Capo Press, 1977.

SEEGER, RUTH CRAWFORD. *American Folk Songs for Children, in Home, School, and Nursery School*. New York: Doubleday and Co., 1948.

SOUTHERN, EILEEN. *The Music of Black Americans: A History*. New York: W. W. Norton, 1971.

SPENCER, CORNELIA. *How Art and Music Speak to Us*. New York: John Day Co., 1963.

STEARNS, MARSHALL W. *The Story of Jazz*. New York: Oxford University Press, 1973.

STROBELL, ADAH PARKER. *Bicentennial Games 'N Fun*. Washington, D.C.: Acropolis Books, 1975.

TUCKER, JO ANNE KLINEMAN. "The Use of Creative Dramatics as an Aid in Developing Reading Readiness with Kindergarten Children." Ph.D. dissertation, University of Wisconsin, 1971.

UNDERHILL, RUTH MURRAY. *Singing for Power*. New York: Ballantine, 1973.

WALSH, GERTRUDE. *Sing Your Way to Better Speech*. New York: E. P. Dutton and Co., 1947.

WARD, WINIFRED. *Playmaking with Children*. New York: Appleton-Century-Crofts, 1957.

WHITE, FLORENCE, and AKIYAMA, KAZUO. *Children's Songs from Japan*. New York: Edward B. Marks Music Corp., 1960.

YOLEN, WILL. *The Complete Book of Kites and Kite Flying*. New York: Simon and Schuster, 1976.

# Index